OBLIVION AND STONE

OBLIVION
AND STONE
■ ■ ■

A SELECTION OF
CONTEMPORARY
BOLIVIAN POETRY
AND FICTION

Selected and Edited by
Sandra Reyes

Translated by
John DuVal,
Gastón Fernández-Torriente,
Kay Pritchett,
and Sandra Reyes

THE UNIVERSITY OF ARKANSAS PRESS
FAYETTEVILLE   1998

Manufactured in the United States of America

02 01 00 99 98 5 4 3 2 1

Designed by Alice Gail Carter

⊗ The paper used in this publication meets the minimum requirements of the American National Standard for Permanence of Paper for Printed Library Materials Z39.48-1984.

LIBRARY OF CONGRESS CATALOGING-IN-PUBLICATION DATA

Oblivion and stone : a selection of contemporary Bolivian poetry and fiction / selected and edited by Sandra Reyes : translated by John DuVal . . . [et al.].
p. cm.
The poetry is in the original Spanish and in English translation; the fiction, in translation only.
ISBN 1-55728-511-X (cloth : alk. paper). — ISBN 1-55728-512-8 (paper : alk. paper)
1. Bolivian literature—20th century—Translations into English.
2. Bolivian poetry—20th century. I. Reyes, Sandra. II. DuVal, John, 1940–
PQ7813.5.035 1998
860.8'0984—DC21 97-51161
CIP

Special thanks to the Partners in America Association for all the coordination and assistance of its members and their contributions to this project. A very special thank you goes out to Nicomedes Suárez Araúz, Gastón Fernández-Torriente, and Edgar Lora, without whose efforts this work could never have come to light. It exists only due to the dedication and hard work of these people.

ACKNOWLEDGMENTS

These poems appeared in the following anthologies.

Indice de la poesia Boliviana contemporana, Juan Quiros, ed., 1984: "En el mar," by Roberto Echazu Navajas; "Apóstrofe," "Desde el negro lagar de los olvidos," and "Yo respondo," by Alcira Cardona Torrico; "Canción de la nueva luna," "Las Prostitutas de Paris," and "Los Pinos de Roma," by Julio de la Vega.

Antologia de la poesia Boliviana, Yolanda Bedregal, ed., 1991: "Poemas," by Rubén Vargas; "Desfloramiento," by Reymi Ferreira; "Poemas," by Antonio Rojas; "Cita," by Eduardo Mitre; "El Toro," by Nicomedes Suárez Araúz; and "Los Campos olvidados," by Jesús Urzagasti.

Poetas contemporaneos de Bolivia, Eduardo Mitre, ed., 1986: "Los Campos olvidados," "Los Que desesperan," and "Una estrella en el bosque," by Jesús Urzagasti; and "Tiwanaku," by Pedro Shimose.

Breve Poesia Cruceña, Tomo I, ed., 1990: "Amor político," by Luis Andrade Sanjines; "Llegó Papá Noel" and "Quisiera arrimarme un poquito," by Renzo Gismondi Zumarán; and "Muchachuela mimosa vestida de nombres," "Los sueños serán sueños," and "Siento haberte esperado," by Freddy Estremadoiro Romero.

Other poems were taken directly from the poetic works listed in the biographical information.

These short stories appeared in the following anthologies of short fiction.

Taller del cuento nuevo, Jorge Suárez, ed., 1986: "Crónica secreta de la guerra del Pacifico," by German Araúz; "La Ley," by Amilkar Jaldín; and "La Luz," by Blanca Elena Paz.

Cuentos bolivianos contemporaneos, Hugo Lijeron Alverdi and Ricardo Pastor, eds., 1991: "La Condenada," by Adolfo Cáceres Romero.

Los mejores cuentos bolivianos del siglo XX, Ricardo Pastor Poppe, ed., 1989: "El forastero y el candelabra de plata," by Gastón Suarez; and "Los Ultimos," by Walter Montenegro.

Other stories were taken from the works of specific authors, as mentioned in the biographical information.

CONTENTS

FICTION

INTRODUCTION

"Oblivion and Stone," the English version of the title of a poem by Eduardo Mitre, are words that can be used to describe the contemporary Bolivian literary effort—words that are symbols of death and at the same time symbols of ceremony; in short, they exemplify the struggle of a country of people to make their name in a world where ceremony and symbol are hard earned.

Contemporary Bolivian writing is realistic, sometimes abstract, but always down-to-earth. Both the poetry and the fiction portray a mature society that has worked its way up in a few centuries' time, over and around the obstacles of an all but uncivilized world, a society that has had to learn to cope with both the painful intrusion and the blessing of technology in a race to keep up with the cultural demands that other societies impose on it. When one reads these excerpts and sketches of Bolivian life, one cannot but find oneself drawn closer to these endearing people who proclaim indulgently and without shame the praises and the secrets of a tough life of loving and giving.

From a critical viewpoint, one might look at the Bolivian writing through a multicultural, analytical viewpoint: as many post-colonial writings have developed through the centuries, so has the Bolivian effort—in an attempt to establish a national identity. It is safe to say that a number of the short stories that are published reflect provincial themes and values, as in Adolfo Cáceres Romero's story, "The Damned," for example. Other trends, however, are political, even anti-political, both in fiction and in poetry, as in the fiction of German Araúz, Oscar Barbery Justiniano, Oscar Barbery Suarez, and many others.

Much of the poetry is introspective, even confessional, at times. Most of it is now being written in free verse, even by those of the older generation of poets, such as Yolanda Bedregal, Raul Otero Reiche, and Oscar Cerruto, who may have started out in more formalistic styles, but who later reverted to freer stylistic modes of expression. Very few Bolivians are adhering to traditional forms now, a fact which could be a statement on their part that those rhetorical styles and structures have proven inadequate to describe the kinds of experiences that they wish to relate. The poetry is heavily symbolic and imagistic, fraught with motifs pertaining to nature and the earth: stones, trees, flowers, grasses, animals, and their respective relationships to the people. Underlying all of the poetic themes and motifs are suppressed and condensed statements and beliefs about the society of the Bolivian people and their plight, as it were, in relation to the powers that be, such as tradition, God, fate, life in general and how it deals with us, and, in some instances, the governing forces of politics and the system. In the fiction as well as the poetry, there is a good-natured attitude of acceptance and awareness, sometimes with a sense of irony, as to what can and cannot be undertaken in a given society's efforts to meet the needs of outside influences within their own culture. Certainly the reformist's voice is there, as the writers recognize problems and see a need for change, but with that there is not necessarily a prevailing sense of anxiety or desperation that would make itself heard.

The work of the younger poets all seems to portray a fresh outlook on their world, poets like Alejandro Mara, Freddy Estremadoiro Romero, Reymi Ferreira, Elias Serrano Pantoja, Beatriz Kuramoto, Antonio Rojas, and Amilkar Jaldín, for example. The poetry of that generation, of those born in the late fifties to the sixties, can be experimental, symbolic, thought-provoking, abstract, and usually quite enjoyable to read, whether one understands it completely or not.

In short fiction, the "short, short" story is very popular, as some authors turn out works of no more than two or three pages in length, the product sometimes having a closer resemblance to a narrative poem than to a story with traditional elements of plot, character, setting, and so on. The result is often abstract and/or experimental, as in Nicomedes Suárez Araúz's *Cuentos de Leon,* in which the prose becomes almost surrealistic or heavily symbolic in quality, or in the short, short stories of Blanca Elena Paz and others. On the other hand, even some of these "postage-stamp" short stories still have enough of the characteristics of fiction to allow them to be classified as such. For our purposes, all those to be found in this anthology are placed in the fiction section simply from having been labeled as stories by their authors.

Novels are not represented in this anthology, but many of the good writers of short fiction, such as Ramon Rocha Monroy and others, have turned their skills toward producing some eloquently turned novels. On the critical spectrum, the novels of Bolivia can be said to range from pole to pole, that is, anywhere from the traditional to the experimental.

Edgar Lora, a well-known critic of the literature of his native country, has said that Bolivian writing has always been a "dynamic and vigorous social discourse." Contemporary Bolivian literature, he maintains, can be "subversive, militant and revolutionary." He asks us not only to examine Bolivia's imminent social, collective memory but also to explore, through both a scientific and subjective viewpoint, the discourse of ideology, in an analysis of the cultural identity created from the myths, the traditions, and the folklore of the society, as a universal projection of the personal vision of the writer.

In speaking of the selections made here for the purpose of this anthology, it is obvious to the reader that not every writer is represented—this is not to say that all were not worthy of including. This anthology is an attempt at a random sampling of the various types of poetry and fiction that have been and are being written in Bolivia today and over the past few decades. It has focused predominantly on living writers. In an effort to define the poetic and prosaic voice of Bolivian writing, this work offers a panoramic view, a diffusion of the Bolivian consciousness in the manifestation of the writers' thoughts, feelings, desires, images, and judgments regarding their own identities.

Speaking for the translations themselves, the translators, myself included, have attempted to keep the original intent of the writer in mind at all times, while maintaining the ever delicate and challenging balance of sensitivity to the poetic or the prosaic effect. Sometimes lines or words have been transposed, and in cases where multiple meanings were possible, choices had to be made. From the viewpoint of a translator, however, these liberties have neither changed the original meanings nor taken away from the possible affective response of the informed reader.

In conclusion, it can be said that this anthology represents the contemporary scene in Bolivian letters, in the special sense that most of these writers are currently at work.

POETRY

LOBA ENEMIGA

Yolanda Bedregal

Loba con dientes de ausencia mordiendo la lejanía,
¡cuanto desgarrón has hecho en mi vestido de fiesta!
Mi recuerdo va lamiendo sumiso por la distancia,
y tu, loba, desafinas hasta el matiz de los versos.
Tus dientes se van cayendo, menudas horas de hueso,
en el sendero que abrían mis pasos a su pradera.
Todo se va marchitando bajo la barrera hostil
de tus dientes duros, loba.
Te has comido el pan suave de mi palabra y mis besos;
te has bebido todo el vino y toda la leche tibia
y la miel de mis ternezas.
Loba—Ausencia, solo traes girones de cartas frias.
¡Pobre de mí! ¡Y pobre loba! No tienes culpa de nada.
Las distancias tienen hambre y devoran el recuerdo.
¡Pobre de mí! ¡Pobre loba!
La distancia . . . los adioses . . . ese camino de olvido.

¡Ven, loba! Bébete tú de mis manos
la sangre de corderito
que yo cuidaba para él.

ENEMY WOLF-BITCH

Yolanda Bedregal

Wolf-bitch with missing teeth biting into the space of distance,
look what you've done to my party dress!
My memory is licking submission through the distance,
and you, Wolf, are all out of tune and off beat with the lines.
Your teeth keep falling, minute moments of bone,
into the footpath that my footprints made in your meadow.
Everything is shriveling beneath the hostile barrier
of your hard teeth, Wolf-bitch.
You've gobbled up all the soft bread of my words, my kisses.
You've drunk all the wine and the warm milk,
all the honey of my tenderness.
Wolf—Absence, you bring only streams of cold letters.
Poor me! Poor Wolf! It's not your fault.
Distances are hungry. They devour memory.
Poor me! Poor Wolf!
The distance . . . the farewells . . . the road of forgetfulness.

Come Wolf. Drink from my hands
the lamb's blood
that I was saving for him.

esas cosas que no tienen nombre
ocultas en la esquina de las sonrisas turbias,
esas palabras sin voz
esas miradas sin ojos, esos contactos extraños:
abrazos que se curvan pesados de fragrancia,
pasos inaudibles que nos desvelan,
esas cosas sin nombre,
¡como me turban sin que existan!
¡como me sangran sin que nazgan!
Van de la noche a la nada.
Saltan del sueño a la vida.

those things that have no name
hidden at the corners of sly smiles,
those voiceless words
those eyeless looks, those strange touches,
curving embraces heavy with perfumey scent,
inaudible steps that keep us wakeful,
those nameless things,
how they confuse me unless they exist!
how they bleed me unless they be born!
They go out into the nothing of the night.
They leap into life out of a dream.

LOS PINOS DE ROMA

Julio de la Vega

Se diría un ejército,
un batallón de paz.
Como una multitud los pinos
pintan la geografía de la ciudad;
¿de qué distancia viene su verde simetría?
¿desde qué punto de la historia
sus paralelas líneas han llegado
a nuestro siglo,
a nuestra época de ruidos?
Yo los he visto erguidos mirar hacia las nubes
cuando los besan los aviones;
en sus extensas copas,
mesas redondas del alivio,
multipicaron nidos,
desde antes de la luz,
desde la cruz y por los siglos de los siglos.
Sobre los siete montes,
en los siete collados de la Ciudad Eterna
he visto despeinarse sus melenas.
Los he mirado hablando a las palmeras
llamarlas compañera vegetal y acariciarlas
y conquistar su talle
con su amplia ramazón de clorofila.

Van todos los caminos hasta Roma
y de Roma partieron los caminos,
así partió el reinado de los pinos;
y ahora en todo bosque,
en todo trompo de la infancia,
en toda rueda de molino,
duerme también la historia,
duerme el imperio verde
y alumbra el bienstar de sus maderas
en la floresta universal . . .

THE PINES OF ROME

Julio de la Vega

You might call them an army,
a battalion of peace.
Like a host of angels, the pines
paint the geography of the city.
From what distance to us
comes their green symmetry?
From what point in history
have their parallel lines
arrived at our age,
in our noisy century?
I have seen them standing upright, gazing at clouds,
kissed by low-flying planes,
and in their outstretched bowers,
round tables of comfort.
Since the beginning
they've produced nests,
since the cross, and for centuries.
Over the seven hills,
on the seven summits of the Eternal City,
I've seen them drop their needles.
I've seen them speaking to the palms
as blood brothers, embracing them,
overtopping them
with their ample supply of greenishness.

All roads go to Rome,
and from Rome all roads depart,
as has the Pine Kingdom.
And now in full forest,
in the full bloom of infancy,
in the full force of the mill wheel,
history also sleeps,
the imperial green sleeps
and in the well-being of its timbers
steeps universal wood . . .

Yo los he visto en claras noches
bajo la luz de las estrellas iluminar la música,
cuando en las horas de Mazencio Beethoven era un dios
y los pinos su guardia . . .

Largas hileras sensitivas
cobijaron sus ramas y consagraron a los pinos
el rubio sol de los domingos . . .

Yo he visto sus siluetas bajo el pincel del Domenechino
quizá desde ese entonces, quizá desde el pretorio,
desde el incendio histórico,
están velando sueños y despertando nupcias
junto a eternas murallas,
desde piadosos himnos.
Sobre los años y las piedras
vienen y pasan sobre el tiempo
y sobre el toldo de los siglos.
Vienen y pasan como aurigas
con su canción los pinos . . .

Yo los he visto en Monte Mario distribuir el alba
como una ronda de alegría
girando al pie de las colinas . . .

Yo los he visto en Porta Pía
en ojivas augustas sublimizar el aire
su resonante Ave María . . .

Cuando el Foro Romano no era ruina
y los mercados de Trajano, vieron pasar las multitudes,
cuando se irguió la piedra y las columnas
y este tiempo pasado era tiempo vivido,
ya se sintió el perfume de los pinos,
ya acarició el antigua oído,
su ronco voz en epinicios . . .

Cuando se calla el ruido,
cuando el Trastevere dormita su proletario esfuerzo cotidiano

On clear nights I've seen them in the starlight
setting music aglow
in the Mazencio hour, when Beethoven was a god
and the pines his guardian . . .

Long, sensitive needles enshroud their branches
sanctifying, for the pines,
the blonde sunbeams of Sundays . . .

I've seen them silhouetted beneath the brush of Domenicino
perhaps since then, perhaps since the praetorian,
since the bonfires of old,
they've been lulling dreams and waking weddings
out of pious hymnals
and from out of eternal walls.
Across the decades and over the stones they come;
they pass through time
over the awnings of the ages.
They come and go like coachmen
with a piney song.

I've seen them on Mount Mario giving out the dawn
in a joyful serenade
throbbing at the mountains' foothills . . .

I've seen them in Porta Pia
in august arches, their resonant Ave Marias
sanctifying the air.

Before the forum was a ruin
and the Trayono marketplace still looked on at crowds passing,
when stones and columns were still being built
and the past was being lived,
people were still breathing the pine perfume,
and the ears of the ancients were caressed
by a rough, hoarse, piney voice.

When the noise stops,
when the lumberjack lays down his proletarian ax,

yo he visto caminar los altos pinos
y perfumar los sueños y acariciar las sábanas
y el pobre dormitorio de los niños;
he sentido sus pasos en la fábrica
y en la hora que descansan los martillos,
los he visto en la fonda de los pobres
bendecir con amor el pan y el vino . . .

El Campidoglio se ilumina con sus nocturnos bichos
y en el momento de los grillos
cuando la tarde dora su crepúsculo estivo,
yo he visto concentrándose a los pinos
para llamar al Angelus,
para encerrar los ruidos
para extender de la montaña
hacia los barrios unto al río,
el manto azul de los siglos . . .

Cuando nació el color
y renació el buril en incontables peristilos,
cuando volcaron luces sobre Roma
con su pincel los florentinos,
en ese tiempo sobre la campiña
inspiraron atmósferas iluminando las pupilas
de los pintores místicos.
Así pasaron sobre el tiempo bebiendo agua del Tíber
acompañando al río en su vuelta de siglos;
pasaron como pasan los marinos
con su canción de los pinos . . .

Ahora son el nuevo ejército
la nueva aurora sobre el mundo viejo,
la espera de la paz,
el reinado de líquenes y el pabellón de enredaderas
y el último jardín de los olivos.
He sentido la historia de los pinos,
los he visto pasar, los estoy viendo
con un manto tendido sobre Roma,
¡y me llevo como un beso sus aromas . . . !

I have seen the tall pines walking.
They caress the sheets and perfume the dreams
in the humble bedrooms of sleeping children.
I've heard their footsteps in the factories
in the resting hour of hammers.
I've seen them in the lodgings of the poor,
giving love blessings to the bread and the wine . . .

When the countryside sparkles with night bugs
in the cricket hour,
when the evening coats its summer twilight with gold,
I've seen the blue cloak of the centuries
settling over the pines,
calling out to Angelus,
locking up noise,
stretching down from the mountains
toward the barrios by the river . . .

When color was born
and engravers' tools were recreated in multi-fashion
and the Florentines made Rome dizzy with light,
then, over the plains
the pines inspired worlds around them,
lighting up the pupils
of the mystic painters.
So they passed through time, drinking the water of the Tiber,
companion of the river in their time trek.
They passed like mariners
with their pine song . . .

Now they're the new army;
a new aurora over an old world,
the hope of peace,
a kingdom of lichens and a pavilion of foliage,
the last Mount of Olives.
I've heard the story of the pines;
I've seen them pass; I see them now
with their mantel spread out over Rome;
I'm carrying their fragrance with me, like a kiss!

CANCIÓN DE LA NUEVA LUNA

Julio de la Vega

Siempre fuiste luna nueva
por la intacta unidad de tu perfil
pero ahora eres renovadamente nueva
porque no eres la misma
contra tu voluntad
sigues rueda en el cosmos
sigues faro antiguo
sigues linterna influyente
en mares y almas
sigues precipicio del cielo
redondel contemplado
desde el hoyo profundo
sigues felina mirando en la noche
o luciérnaga gigante,
pero,
sobre tu blanco delantal hay manchas
de sangre que todavía no es
salpicaduras llegadas desde abajo
alfileres de corbata portando telas dibujadas
hirieron tus mejillas
grabándote estrellas y martillos sobre el rostro
falenas en tu mar sin aguas y tu vientre acústico.
Los sabios de este mundo
garabatean fórmulas sobre tu cara de papel
y enormes patas electrónicas se asientan
encima de tu piel
repitiendo el ademán grosero o
de colocar los pies sobre los escritorios
como queriendo desatar en ti
lo que en la tierra estaba atado.
Besan tu superficie
heroicos espíritus de hombres
adelantados de mar
en la posesión de tu alma estructura

SONG OF THE NEW MOON

Julio de la Vega

You were always a new moon
from the intact unity of your profile
but now you are newly renewed
because you've changed
against your will
you go on, a wheel in the cosmos
you go on, an ancient lighthouse
you go on, penetrating beacon
in seas and souls
you go on, precipice of heaven
studied orb
from the deep abyss
you go on, feline, or giant firefly,
watching in the night
but there are stains
on your white mantel,
stains of blood that is yet to be
spatterings from down here below
tiepins tacked to patterned cloth
wounding your cheeks
stars and hammers engraved across your countenance
night moths in your waterless sea and your acoustic belly.
The wise ones of this world
scribble formulas over your paper face
and enormous electronic feet plant themselves
upon your skin
repeating the awkward gestures
of positioning their feet over the desks
as if trying to unloose in you
whatever was tied up on earth below.
Kissing your surface
are the heroic spirits of men
let loose from the sea
to possess the structure of your soul.

que explotarán un reino de miradas
de suspiros en órbita
lanzados hacia ti como aerolitos
por muchachas de todas las épocas.
Explotarán un reino de intenciones del hombre
de igualrse a los astros en su vuelo;
de perlas ingrávidas de color celeste
de escarapelas descoloridas por el tiempo
de escafandras que te cayeron
después de vueltas millonarias
por los espacios siderales
de estalagtitas que fueron
pensamientos congelados al vacío
y subidos por invisibles escaleras
desde el furor de la gente terrestre
de sus noches en vela bajo tu lampo
por saber cómo se podría
ir a ponerte en sombra de una pantalla mecánica
o colocarte un puente levadizo hacia el espacio
o un hombre en tu ojo fumando un cigarrillo
o un par de anteojos
para que nos mires,
además de alumbrarnos
o una casa sin cimiento,
suspendida, inmóvil
o hacer días con tus noches
o jugar una partida de naipes
con ladrillos pintados
sin lágrimas
para que no le caigan nubes a tu atmósfera
y con nuevas palabras
que no están en diccionarios
para que los hombres que lleguen hasta ti
y en lo futuro vivan
colgados de los bordes de tu orla
puedan lograr lo que en la tierra no lograron:
intercambiar sus almas
mediante soplos que se vuelvan tubos sólidos

They will explode a kingdom of stars
and sighs bursting into orbit
hurled against you like meteorites
by little girls of every era.
They will explode a kingdom of men's intentions
equal to astros in flight, a cascade
of pearls engraved with celestial color
of cockades, rosettes faded with time
of spacesuits falling from your orbit
after millions of cycles
through sidereal space
of stalactites that were
thoughts frozen into the void
suddenly, through invisible stairways,
from the furor of terrestrial folk
at their night-watches, beneath your lamp,
by knowing how it could be done:
to go and put you in the shadow of a mechanical screen
or make you a bridge out into space
or a man in your eye smoking a cigarette
or a pair of glasses
so you can look at us
as well as illuminate us,
or a house without foundation
suspended, motionless,
or make days of your nights
or play a game of cards
with painted bricks
with no tears
so that clouds do not fall into your atmosphere
and with new words
not found in dictionaries
so that the men who reach you
and live in the future
dangling from the fringes of your embroidery
can achieve what was not achieved on earth
an interchanging of the souls
while breaths solidify into tubes

y escucharse mutuamente
por cuanto la esperanza será un cuerpo
que pueda apisonarse
como un barco concreto
y la tolerancia será espejo
donde se mire uno y se refleje el otro
y la igualdad
será tu misma, inspiradora forma,
convertida en un plato para todos,
y la hermandad será una subida juntos
todos colgados de una larga sábana
que desde la tierra hasta tu beso lleve
y la fe será saber que aun esta hazaña es poco
para igualarnos con quien te puso
como una medallas sin cadena
en el medio del cosmos.

Siempre será tan nueva como ahora
porque la pureza invadida
sólo puede originar mayor pureza.

listening respectively one to another
whereby hope may become a body
that could press down
like a concrete barge
and tolerance become a mirror
where one looks and another is reflected
where equality
will be your very self, inspirational form,
converted into a dish for all the world
and brotherhood will be a sudden leap together
all hanging from one long sheet
stretching from your kiss down to earth
and faith will be the knowledge that all this is nothing
if we compare ourselves to the one who put you there
hanging like a chainless medallion
in the middle of the cosmos.

You will always be as new as you are now
for your ravaged purity
can only give birth to a greater pureness.

ROJO ATARDECER

Germán Coimbra Sanz

Entre los brazos del río
un cielo rojo y violeta
se desmenuza en cristales
que giran sobre la arena.
Los arboles de la orilla
extenden sus ramas negras
y cuelgan sobre las aguas
contorsionadas culebras.
Sigo adelante. El caballo
endereza por la senda
que desenvuelve su rumbo
hacia el Poniente. En la selva,
llena de sombras, crepitan
a pasar las hojas secas.
Canta un pájaro en la fronda
una canción de leyenda.
En un claro del camino
se recorta una palmera
y mas allá hay una casa
medio oculta en la floresta.
Como por encargo laten
los perros en la tranquera,
hasta que la lejanía
y el silencio los sosiega.
Allí termina el sendero
y comienza la pradera:
rojos celajes arriba
y un mar oscuro en la tierra.
De pronto rompe el silencio
un disparo de escopeta . . .
Ya es de noche. El caballo
se abre paso entre la hierba.

RED NIGHTFALL

Germán Coimbra Sanz

Between the river's arms
a red and purple sky
shatters into crystals
that sigh over the sand.
The trees along the riverbank
stretch out their black branches
hanging over the water
like writhing serpents.
I keep on.
The horse picks his way
along the path that winds its course
toward the west. In the underbrush,
heavy with shadows,
dry leaves crackle at our passing.
A bird in the fronds is singing
a song of legends.
At the road's clearing
there's a silhouette of a palm
and farther on a house
half-hidden in the thicket.
As if on command
dogs begin barking
in the doorway until the distance
and the silence quiet them.
There the path ends
and the meadow begins.
Red-streaked sky above
and a dark ocean of land.
Suddenly the silence is broken
by the crack of a rifle shot . . .
It is night. The horse forges his way
through the tall grass.

LA TARDE

Germán Coimbra Sanz

Oro blanco y verde oro
en el patio de hojas nuevas.
Orquideas que mece el viento
sobre columpios de cuerdas.
Viento, viento, viento, viento
con remolinos de arena.
Sol rayado con los trinos
de cristalinas saetas.
Parpadean los postigos
y los portones se cierran.
La tarde tiende su hamaca
para dormir en la siesta.
Viene un aire de nostalgia
desde oscuras alacenas:
olor o pinas maduras,
a chocolate chocolate y canela,
y en las orillas del sueño
la tarde sus ojos cierra,
como si se los besaran
los labios de una morena.

THE AFTERNOON

Germán Coimbra Sanz

White gold and green gold
on the patio of new leaves.
Orchids tremble in the wind
over columns of vines.
Wind, wind, wind, wind
with tiny whirlpools of sand.
Sunrays streaked in triplets
of crystalline needles.
The shutters flap and bang;
the inner doors slam shut.
The afternoon stretches out its hammock
to take a siesta.
An air of nostalgia wafts through
from within dark pantries:
aromas of ripe pineapple,
of cinnamon and chocolate,
while on the banks of a dream
the afternoon closes its eyes
as if to be kissed
by the lips of a dark woman.

YO RESPONDO

Alcira Cardona Torrico

Dadme tan sólo el punto en que descubra
el eje de la vida
y os daré la razón de toda hechura.

Poblaré la existencia
de alegría.
Anudaré los vientos,
extenderé las ramas,
dejaré encendida
la luz mas leve
para el mejor paisaje.
Asularé de brisas
el estanque.
Encenderé la luna
y diré:
—el mundo es la verdad
en que palpitan,
el corazón del sol,
la fe del santo,
y el espíritu bueno de la hormiga—

Pero antes,
dadme la razón en que descubra
el eje de la vida.
Solo encuentro senderos sin holgura
que dudan

y retornan y se oxidan.

I ANSWER

Alcira Cardona Torrico

Give me only that point of discovery
of the axis of life
and I'll give the science and reason of craft.

I'll populate life with joy.
I'll knot up the winds,
I'll stretch out the branches,
I'll leave the most weightless
light burning
for the best landscape.
I'll blue the ponds
with zephyrs.
I'll light up the moon
and I'll say:
The world is truth
in which beats the sun's heart,
the faith of the saint,
and the good spirit of the ant—

But first,
give me the reason of discovery
of the axis of life.
I find only narrow pathways
doubtful,

doubling back and rusting.

APOSTROFE

Alcira Cardona Torrico

Y un día,
Señor de los apóstrofes audaces
llegándose al dolor, dijo a los placidos:
—Oídme todos, con desnudez y sed,
¡y sin disfraces!

Porque sangre
que nunca mas goteada,
ya coágulo indeleble, mi verso,
será para los que me lean, noche amarga.

Con Dios en la punta de los dedos,
escrito con los ojos y el oído,
abultarán el llanto,
y entonces se sentirá terror de haber nacido.
No me leáis en fresco atardecer
junto al gentio.

Léedme
cuando os quemen las vísceras en la noche de espanto
cuando sintáis sobre los hombros
la viga que os cargaron por esclavos.
Ni con madre, con hijos, con esposa me busquéis;
léedme sollozando,
que hay tedio y cólera en mi ser,
y miedo
de llevar adherido este mal rostro
hast el final del tiempo . . .

Aranas del olvido tejerán las pupilas
de ojos muertos que abrazan el silencio,
y con ellas, yo traeré hasta vuestras sonrisas
el desastre del cuerpo.

APOSTROPHE

Alcira Cardona Torrico

And one day
The Lord of bold apostrophes,
approaching pain, said to the meek:
"Hear me, all you naked and thirsty
and undisguised!

For blood
that will never spill again
is clotting within me, unseeable, my song
will be for those who read me, bitterest night.

With God at my fingertips
it's written with sound and sight,
they'll let loose a mighty howl
and feel terror at being born.
Don't read me in the calm cool of evening
out in the crowd.

Read me
when you feel the scorch of the molten sludge of hideous night,
when you feel bearing down on your shoulders
the heavy yoke that claims you as its slaves.
Don't come looking for me with mothers, with sons, with wives;
read me sobbing,
for there's agony and rage in my being
and fear
of wearing this evil face glued to me
until the end of time . . .

Spiders of oblivion will web up the pupils
of dead eyes that caress the silence,
and with them I'll bring disaster of the body
right up to your smiling faces.

Mi palabra,
látigo del hambre repartida
en preguntas de horror sobre los músculos,
repiterá terrible hasta los truenos:

¿Cuya es mi vida?

Contestarán los nervios contraídos
de afiebrado hospital,
cuando mentida paciencia de enfermeras
hiera
el último suspiro de la angustia final.

Entonces, serán bronca mi voz, mis pies de fuego,
sin hora para ver, sin el silencio
para sentir y comprender
el ritmo
de todo lo que existe y lo que pasa,
lo que llega girando en círculos oscuros
al cerebro del mal.

Ya es tarde, os diré.
En las trenzas gitanas, en las manos guerreras
agazapada
está la muerte, en las plazas y fiestas.

Y vosotros, y aquellos que extendieron la mano,
recibido ya el pago,
os marcharéis aleves y cobardes,
dejándome en silencio cabizbaja y burlada.

Tan solo quedaré yo,
con las costillas clavadas en el alma,
y mi sangre,
ya coágulo en mi verso, para los que me lean,
será en el infinito, ¡noche amarga!

My word,
a hungry whip
cracked in inquisitions of horror over the limbs,
will lash thunderously over and over, repeating:

'Whose life is mine?'

Contracted nerves will answer
from an enfevered hospital
where the lying patience of nurses
wounds
the last sigh of final anguish.

Then, my voice, my flaming feet will be rage
without the time to see, without the silence
to feel and comprehend
the rhythm
of all that exists and passes,
all that comes whirling in dark circles
to the evil brain.

It's too late now, I'll tell you.
In the gypsy camps, in warriors' hands
in the fiestas and the village squares,
death is squatting.

And all you, those who've held out your hands,
you've already been paid.
You'll march out of here, traitors and cowards,
leaving me silent, scorned, my head bowed.

And I'll stay, terribly alone,
my ribs nailcd to my soul,
my blood
clotting in my songs; for those who read me,
it will be infinity, bitterest night!"

DESDE EL NEGRO LAGAR DE LOS OLVIDOS

Alcira Cardona Torrico

Desde el negro lagar de los olvidos
manchado vino
me ofreció el cansancio;
—muere—dijeron
las voces de la angustia
¡y no morí bebiéndome un calvario!

FROM THE BLACK LAGOON OF OBLIVION

Alcira Cardona Torrico

From the black lagoon of oblivion
weariness offered me
tainted wine.
"Die," said all the voices of the Furies.
But I didn't die—
I drank myself into a stupor!

LA CAIDA

Jorge Suárez

No es la caída lenta de las hojas,
ni el estrepito azul de los metales,
ni el fragor de las piedras.
No deja en torno suyo la rosa de la sangre,
ni el jardín de las vísceras expuesto
sobre las avenidas.
Gravita en sí, callada,
sin gravedad, sin peso,
repercute en si misma,
conmociona su propia levedura.
Fuera mejor que tenga su pólvora precisa,
su claro fulminante,
para dejarnos rotos,
cadaveres ausentes de su caída eterna.
Ni siquiera es la muerte . . .
Porque a veces forjamos alrededor de un sueño
la meta de los vuelos
y el límite del agua,
sobre nimia ternura
proclamamos la música
total del universo,
en la punta de un ala sustentamos
monumentos de plomo.
Pero se apaga el sueño,
se apaga la ternura,
se va el aire, se va
sin acordarse,
se va el viento, se va,
y se va sin llevarse
los árboles crecidos.
No es la caída lenta de las hojas.
Es el árbol interno
que devora su propio laberinto de pájaros.
No es el fragor azul de los metales.

THE FALLING

Jorge Suárez

It's not the slow falling of leaves,
nor metals' blue clashing,
nor stones' shattering.
It does not leave roses of blood in its wake,
nor gardens of thick vines
trailing over the avenues.
It gravitates from within itself, hushed;
without gravity, weightless,
it rebounds within,
bubbles in its own ferment,
better to have its own fuse
detonator, bomb
for us to be left broken,
corpses absent from our own eternal falling.
Nor is it death, even . . .
For sometimes we forge, around a daydream,
the goal of the flights
and the limitations of water;
with excessive tenderness
we proclaim the total
music of the universe;
tottering idols of lead,
we balance ourselves on a wingtip.
But the dream snuffs out,
tenderness snuffs out
and wind goes away;
it goes away,
it leaves without recall,
without taking with it
the mature trees.
It is not the slow falling of leaves.
It's the inner tree
devouring its own labyrinth of birds.
It's not the blue metals' clashing.

El corazón, andarivel profundo,
bota su carga y vuelve a recogerla
sobre su propio abismo.
Luego vienen los siglos del minuto, sin tregua.
En un segundo vasto que el tiempo diafaniza
repercuten los años y los días
y transcurren los aros solares y las lunas
y los círculos negros y los círculos claros
que preceden al vertigo;
luego somos un turbio farol que se desploma
en los ámbitos solos
de un ciudad desierta.

The heart, deep, beating anvil,
dumps its cargo and comes back to reclaim it
over its own bottomless pit.
Later come the centuries of minutes, without cease-fire.
In a timeless second where time becomes transparent
years and days rebound,
sunbeams and moonbeams fade away,
circles of light and dark
preceding vertigo.
Afterwards we remain, troubled lighthouses, sagging
alone in the circuits
of a deserted city.

LAS PROSTITUTAS DE PARIS

Jorge Suárez

Un río de ternura son,
un bosque de humanas sensaciones,
un rebaño de heridas.
¿A dónde va este mar,
esta bandera hecha de negras faldas,
esta bandada rubia,
este horizonte de zapatos y medias,
esta playa donde han dormido todos . . . ?

Las prostitutas de París pueblan la noche.
¿Qué noche de Walpurgis han nacido?
¿Qué brujo,
qué fauno desbocado, en qué momento,
escribió sobre sus rubios vientres
el amor sin amor, como castigo . . . ?

Las prostitutas de París pueblan la noche,
con sus pequeñas boinas,
con sus blusas perennes.
Asoman taconeando desde lejos
con sus piernas de frío,
llenando de acordeones las esquinas.

Golondrinas nocturnas,
magnolias entreabiertas,
su perfume barato sopla en los bulevares
y se horada la noche de luceros
porque en sus dientes y en sus lenguas
hay una azul fosforescencia,
una sonrisa hecha de sal,
una lágrima oculta;
porque todas fueron también Sonia
y Magdalena y Margarita
y la santa legión de barcos lúgubres
buscando el puerto del amor . . .

34

THE WHORES OF PARIS

Jorge Suárez

They're a river of tenderness,
a forest of human sensation,
a herd of wounds.
Where does this sea go,
this banner of black skirts,
this blonde flock,
this aurora of shoes and stockings,
this beach that everyone has slept on?

The whores of Paris people the night.
What night of Walpurgis have they spawned?
What warlock,
what mouthless fauna? At what moment
did he inscribe on their blonde bellies
love without love, as a punishment?

The whores of Paris people the night,
with their little berets
and their perennial blouses.
The tapping of their heels sounds from far off,
with their icy legs
filling the street corners with an accordion music.

Nocturnal swallows,
half-open magnolia blooms,
their cheap perfume wafts down the boulevards
and the night is pierced with lights,
for in their teeth and tongues
gleams a blue phosphorescence,
a smile made of salt,
a hidden tear,
for all of them were also Sonia
and Mary Magdalene and Margaret
and all the holy legion of mournful barges
searching for the harbor of love . . .

Son las de todo el mundo,
son éstas de París,
estas siluetas,
estos tacones altos bajo medias de malla . . .

Están sobre los puentes
igual que orugas abrigándose,
como mendigos implorando.
Cuerpos en donde cada huella
viene a borrar antiguas huellas,
en este mapa digital que son,
en este plato colectivo,
en este horror que muerden todos.

Hormigas de la noche
van como los *clochards*
con una música mordiendo;
un acordeón inmaterial guía sus pasos,
su errante sucesión de trasnochadas,
su actitud cotidiana de deshojar ventanas
y avenidas nocturnas.

Cuando aparece el alba huyen despavoridas,
la luz del día taladra sus pestañas de plomo
que el pecado del mundo no deja descansar.
Sus cabezas caídas
están soñando almohada propia.

Pero la calle grita
en cuanto el día arrasa las basuras
y la escoba del orden se las lleva
entre papeles,
entre cáscaras,
entre detritus,
entre hojas secas;
ruedan bajo municipales aguas
que limpian el olor a la miseria
y la miseria queda intacta.

these of Paris
are the ones from the whole world,
these silhouettes,
these high heels over their mesh stockings . . .

There they are over the bridges
just like caterpillars, cloaking themselves,
like beggars, imploring.
Bodies in which each fingerprint
comes to erase other former prints
in this digital finger-map that they become,
in this collective dish,
in this horror that everyone has bitten into.

Ants of the night,
they go like bell-ringers
with a biting music;
a metaphysical accordion guides their steps,
their errant succession of night-crossings,
their daily policies of stripping bare the windows
and night alleys.

At dawn-breaking they flee, vaporized,
the light of day stabs their leaden eyelashes
which the sins of the world never let rest,
their fallen heads
dreaming on their pillows.

But the street cries out
as soon as the day cleans up its trash
and the ordering broom carries them away
among the papers,
among the husks and shells,
among the debris
and the dry leaves;
they roll beneath municipal waters
that cleanse the odor of misery
and misery remains intact.

¡Ah! ¡Topos sin guarida!
¡ah! ¡Mariposas tristes con el vuelo prohibido!

La universal concupiscencia dice:
"París es capital de prostitutas"
y grita en bocanada de monedas:
"Pagamos el placer,
ese pequeño saldo de ternura,
ese ancestral estrujamiento lo pagamos,
las desvestimos pero les pagamos."

Sí.
Pagan el desvestido pero no pagan el vestido,
ni el tren de noches en la esquina,
ni el pie mojándose en la nieve,
ni el látigo del viento en sus rodillas,
ni el beso del invierno helándose los senos.
Pero la noche vuelve
y reverbera en luz la calle
y el triunfo de la noche es la luciérnaga
y hay un carcaj de luz por todas partes
y se prolonga el día;
porque es sin fin este jolgorio,
este violín tocando el hueco de la noche
y resonando siempre veinticuatro y veinticuatro
y siempre veinticuatro horas.

Montparnasse y Montmartre
La Bastille, Sebastopol,
Pigalle, La Madeleine,
la Rue Lyon
son una sola luz.
un solo baile en una sola noche.
Cuando ellas aparecen para aumentar la población nocturna,
para ahuyentar a los espectros,
parecen una manada pura,
una triunfal concentración dándole gracias a la vida,
porque parecen alegrarse cuando perfuma su *Viens, chéri.*

Oh, moles without a den!
Ah! Sad moths forbidden to fly!

The universal consciousness says:
"Paris is the whore capital"
and cries out in a jangling of coins:
"We pay for the pleasure,
that little settlement of tenderness,
that ancestral squeezing, we pay for it,
we strip them, we disrobe them, but we pay them."

Yes.
They're paid for the disrobing but not for the new garments,
nor for the nightly train on the corner,
nor the feet slushing through the snow,
nor the beating of the wind against the knees,
nor winter's kiss freezing their breasts.
But night returns
and reverberates the streets with light . . .
and the triumph of the night is the streetlight
and there's a holster of light all around,
prolonging the day,
for this merriment is endless,
this violin, playing in the hollow of the night,
resounding always twenty-four and twenty-four
and again twenty-four hours.

Montparnasse and Montmartre,
La Bastille, Sebastopol,
Pigalle, La Madeleine,
the Rue Lyon
are all one single light,
one single dance on a single night.
When they appear to supplement the night population,
to frighten away the phantoms,
they resemble a pure stream,
a triumphal concentration giving thanks to life,
for they seem happy when it perfumes their "Viens, Cheri."

Pero detrás de sus senos
está la historia de París,
bajo sus faldas se oculta todo el dolor del mundo;
por eso el ambulante acordeonista vuelca canciones para ellas
y hay un cartel de luz que no se ve
pero que escrito está sobre los siglos:
¡las prostitutas de París son como un río
que el mundo sorbe y deja helar de frío . . . !

But behind their breasts
the history of Paris lies;
beneath their skirts is hidden all the pain of the world.
No wonder the walking accordionist churns out kind songs for them
and there is a cartel of light that can't be seen
but is written across all the centuries:
the whores of Paris are a river
that the world sips from and leaves freezing in the cold!

EN EL MAR

Roberto Echazu Navajas

1.

En el mar,
hombres colmados de tristeza, cargaban sus fúsiles en el cielo.

2.

Levantaban castillos de victoria
en el azur de la justicia.

3.

La muerte no tiene cuerpo cuando se defiende
no solamente la vida.

4.

Mujeres y niños, hombres y viejos,
morían alegremente.
La fealdad los llenó de alegría
ya madura la muerte.

5.

Los que buscan tesoros en la disculpa injusta
tienen mas palabras con que callar la vergüenza.

6.

Sobre la miseria de su orgullo
edificaron el porvenir.

7.

Para amar lloraban, para morir reían,
el sacrificio de todos los tiempos.

8.

El Amor, la muerte, tienen idéntica confianza:
la dicha y el coraje de vivir como se pueda,
y la muerte que comparte
lo mejor que la vida.

9.

El odio que desata derrota y fracasó,
la sangre que construye victoria y porvenir.
Ya no dudemos de la inocencia de los hombres
cuando se ven mezclados, cómplices de una misma aurora.

IN THE SEA

Roberto Echazu Navajas

I.
In the sea,
men weighed down with sadness were firing missiles into the sky.
2.
They were raising up castles of victory
in the azure blue of justice.
3.
Death has no body when
not only life is defended.
4.
Women and children, young men and old
were dying happily.
Loyalty filled them with joy;
now death ripens.
5.
Those who look for treasures in undeserved forgiveness
have more words with which to hush shame.
6.
Over the misery of their pride
they built the future.
7.
To love, they had to cry; to die, they had to laugh:
the sacrifice of all time.
8.
Love, death; both with the same certainty:
luck and the courage to live as best they can
and death that takes
the best share of life.
9.
It's hatred that lets loose defeat and failure,
blood that builds victory and the future.
We no longer doubt the innocence of men
when we see them mixed together, sharers of one same dawn.

MURAL DEL TIEMPO

Pedro Shimose

Esta es nuestra casa
sin ventanas.
El mal tiempo supura en las paredes.
Se nos muere la tierra.

Ya no sé ni como ocurre que me acuerdo todavía
de nosotros.
Somos de aquí
y de ninguna parte.

MURAL OF TIME

Pedro Shimose

This is our house
without windows.
Foul weather vanquishes the walls.
The land is dying on us.

I don't even know how it is that I can remember it all,
about us.
We are from here.
And from nowhere.

LA CASA DE LA MONEDA

Pedro Shimose

En potosi

Una mascara se rie.
¿De qué se rie?

He llegado a pensar
que todo esto es una broma.

En el patio
los leones soportan
la música del agua.

Y un tintineo de plata
me aturde
bajo un cielo vacio de colores.

El viento bate las ventanas.

Y yo soy otro:
multitad diferente
defensora
del fuego.

THE MONEY HOUSE

Pedro Shimose

In Potosi

A mask is laughing.
What does it laugh about?

I've come to believe
it's all a joke.

On the patio
the lines endure
the water's music.

A tinkling of coins
startles me
beneath a colorless sky.

The wind beats the windows.

And I am another:
a different crowd,
defender
of fire.

TIWANAKU

Pedro Shimose

Tu nombre amarillea,
     oscurece y
          cae,
gastado,
al fondo de la piedra.
         Todo es muerte en ti,
figuración del tiempo,
         muerte que no acaba
  de morir,
         muerte en la lucha a muerte
con tus dioses
         y tus ángeles de piedra.
   Profundo,
     el sueño de la piedra
intenta definirte
pero el frío
     se filtra por tus ojos,
     se hace noche en ti,
   tristeas,
  tus siglos son escombros,
tu sombra
se derrumba
         a cada instante,
se agrieta
     a cada instante,
se desploma en el polvo
     a cada instante.
         Tu funeral
camina
    por telarañas y tormentas.
    El olor de la muerte
      te persigue:
tu escarcha envejecida,
    tu paciencia arrugada,

TIWANAKU

Pedro Shimose

Your name yellows
      darkens
            falls
spent,
at the foot of the stone.
            All is dead in you,
time's configuration,
            death that never stops
   dying,
            death in a struggle with death
with your gods
            and your stone angels.
   Deep,
     the dream of the stone
tries to define you
but the cold
     filters through your eyes,
     turns to night inside you,
   you sadden,
  your centuries are rubbish,
your shadow
crumbles away
            moment by moment,
splitting and cracking
     moment by moment,
tumbling to the dust
     moment by moment.
            Your funeral
treads
   through cobwebs and storms.
   The smell of death
     chases you:
your aging rime,
   your wrinkled patience,

tu círculo,
    tus sellos.

Ya no estás
    piedra vencida, ciega,
piedra de soledad,
        te estás muriendo,
piedra demolida,
        de la noche a la noche
        tu nombre es nada,
piedra sometida,
piedra de silencio
piedra.

your circle,
    your eyebrows.

You are no more
    you blind, conquered stone,
stone of loneliness,
      you're dying,
demolished stone,
      from night into night—
      your name is nothing.
Vanquished stone
silent stone
stone.

DESPUES DE LA MADERA

Pedro Shimose

Algo falta en esta mesa.

No son las flores
        ni las frutas.
¿Donde está el guitarrero,
            el de la voz profundo?

Dejó una nota, diciendo:

"He perdonado todo.
Mataron a mi hermano.
        Me quemaron
                el azucar.
        Me talaron
                el arbol.
                Sembraron de sal
                    mi tierra.
¿Cómo quieres que olvide?"

En el
aire
mi vida
escrita
está.
        Mi libro son estas cicatrices;
este ojo
        que casi ya no ve;
esta sombra
        que camina
                    a trompicones
            sobre charcos
                    de sangre.
Sólo el que ama conoce.
Y sólo el que sueña, permanece.

AFTER THE WOOD

Pedro Shimose

Something is missing at the table.

It's not the flowers
      or the fruit.
  Where's the guitarist,
      the one with the deep voice?

He left a note; it said:

"I've forgiven all.
They killed my brother.
    They burned
        my cane fields.
    They ravaged
        my trees.
        They sowed my planting fields
        with salt.
How am I supposed to forget?"

In the
air
my life
is
written.
    These scars are my book,
this eye
    that scarcely can see,
this shadow
      that walks
           stumbling
      over the coals
           of blood.
Only the one who loves knows.
Only the one who dreams remains.

Amar, sufrir, soñar, vivir, acaso.
Ser hombre, sabiendo que soy río
(río de muerte por donde voy
  casi ahogándome).

De mañanita cuento
las semillas de
cacao, arde
la pajarería en la floresta
    ¿Dónde está el guitarrero?
Se fue oaliente y vuelve casi frío,
emerge del silencio
    como una flor insomne.

Sólo el que ama conoce.

De nuevo estoy aquí,
          pero me llevan.
    "¡Madre, defiéndeme!"
Y no hay padre ni madre en este exilio.
Y yo
estoy
lejos
    sin luna pueblerina,
          sin pero que valga,
              olvidado de todo,
                  casi piedra,
apenas,
un arpegio,
    una canción de amor
al despuntar
    el alba.
Sólo el que sueña, permanece.

Loving, suffering, dreaming, perhaps living,
to be a man, knowing I'm a river
(a river of death wherever I go,
   nearly drowning).

In the early morning I count
the cocoa beans;
the haystacks
burn in the forest.
      Where is the guitarist?
He left hot and he comes back almost cold,
emerging out of the silence
      like an insomniac flower.

Only the one who loves knows.

I'm back again,
            but they're carrying me away.
      "Mother, defend me!"
But there is no father or mother in this exile.
And I,
I am
far
      with no village moon,
            nothing to honor me,
                  forgotten by all,
                        almost a stone,
barely
an arpeggio,
      a love song
at the breaking
      of dawn.
Only the one who dreams remains.

LOS CAMPOS OLVIDADOS

Jesús Urzagasti

Una voz largo tiempo oculta en los árboles
me habla de los sagrados sentimientos, de la copa azul,
cuando la humedad desciende a la Tierra amada.
Quizás llueve mansamente, quizás amo todavía
las tiernas maneras que tiene la vida conmigo.
Camino torpemente nombrado, no me dejes
y deja que alumbre tu misterio con mi voz ciega.
Me acerco al final cierto y la unidad me abraza
aunque nada llevo en las manos
ni la belleza que apacienta los secretos de la Tierra
ni aquel canto que en su sollozo la juventud me prometiera.
Desde un día nocturno te habla mi corazón.
Caen los frutos a su tiempo en la placida tierra.
Lo vivido ha engendrado una criatura desconocida
y mi pecho se rompe por su impulso cristalino
y le ofrece el silencio que gobierna a los astros.

THE FORGOTTEN FIELDS

Jesús Urzagasti

A voice in the trees long-time hidden
speaks to me of sacred sentiments, of the blue goblet
when the wetness descends to dear Earth.
Perhaps its raining thickly, perhaps I'm still in love
with the tender manners life has with me.
Obscenely labeled, I walk; don't leave me,
let your mystery illuminate with my blind voice.
I'm approaching final certainty; unity embraces me
though I have nothing in my hands;
not the beauty inspiring Earth's secrets,
nor that song youth promised me, sobbing.
My heart speaks to you from out of a nocturnal day.
On the placid earth, fruits fall in their time.
The brilliance has spawned an unknown creature,
and my breast bursts from the crystalline force of it,
offering it the star-governing silence.

LOS QUE DESESPERAN

Jesús Urzagasti

Los que desesperan deben reinar en las tinieblas
para encontrar aquella mano del verano que aulla
y cruza el mundo irredento. En ese gesto que la noche oculta
esta abreviado para siempre el secreto de la plenitud.
Caro amigo sojuzgando por el misterio de la luz
y por la temprana adolescencia de una mujer que se perdió en el alba
desde el fondo de aquellos ojos privados de elocuencia
te alaba un aroma nacido para seducir al dragón de la belleza.
Esta soledad es el primer engaño. Este silencio enseña
que lo perdurable tiene sal y llanto llegados del sol negro.

Ya no es la juventud la que habla en los árboles muertos
es el destino que se ha endurecido en tu pecho
como unas fiera que al fin hallo sosiego y emblema.
Calla ante tu única y firme estrella. Que lo porvenir
encuentre que nada ha cambiado en la vieja morada
ni el asombro ni la gracia de permanecer abierto a los desastres.

THOSE WHO DESPAIR

Jesús Urzagasti

Those who despair should reign in darkness
to find that hand of truth that goes howling
across the iridescent world. In motion, hidden by night
the secret of plenitude is abbreviated for all time.
Dear friend overwhelmed by light's mystery,
by the early blooming of a woman lost
in the first flush of day, an aroma is singing
your praises, a fragrance born to seduce the dragon of beauty.
This loneliness is the first deception. This silence teaches
that the eternal is full of salt and tears, sent from a black sun.
It is no longer my youth that speaks in the black trees.

It is destiny: hardened in your breast,
and like a jungle cat, it has finally found solace and symbol.
It hushes before your one firm star. May the future discover
that nothing has changed at the old lodging,
not even the terror nor the blessing of vulnerability to disaster.

UNA ESTRELLA EN EL BOSQUE

Jesús Urzagasti

Solo entendí al universo enceguecido por la eternidad
cuando miré los árboles detenidos como un don en el alba
mientras un animal subterráneo consumido por la nostalgia
se convertía en plegaria en provincia en el fantasma
que debía alcanzarme su mano formada por la primavera.
La sangre ahora reconoce en el horizonte iluminado
el caballo sumergido en su llanto al obediente símbolo
que buscaba en la piedra estelar el habitante nocturno.
Como una leyenda amanece la tierra en la morada muda.
Triunfan sobre la realidad y desaparecen las flores negras
la violencia ejercida para que lo sagrado se inscribiera
en mi pecho apartando la melodia transitoria de la muerte.
Árboles fueron los que me recomendaron mirar al mundo
recobrar su esplendor y devolverle su unidad con mi silencio.

A STAR IN THE FOREST

Jesús Urzagasti

I only understood the universe blind, blinded by eternity
until I looked up at the trees, held back like a gift in the dawn of day
while some underground animal, overcome with nostalgia,
became a prayer-chime, a province, a phantom
that had to come close to me, its hand formed by the springtime.
Now the blood in the illumined horizon
recognizes the horse buried in his moan to the obedient symbol,
in search of the nocturnal dweller in the stellar stone.
Like a legend, it threatens the earth with a purple molting.
Black flowers conquer reality and disperse
violence done, so that sacredness be inscribed on my breast,
tearing loose the fleeting melody of death.
It was the trees who commanded me to look at the world,
to recapture its splendor and give it back its unity with my silence.

CITA

Eduardo Mitre

Cielos, siglos antes
de ahora,
ya veniamos
a la luz de esta manana.
Tú, por un rosario
de palomas
milagrosamente
encadenadas. Yo,
por una rama
de halcones
con nostalgia.
Ya veniamos.
Ya venía la piedra
a ser esquina,
el agodón
tu falda.
Así es, amor, así
y, sin embargo,
no nos salva. No nos
salva de manana.
No nos salva
la sonrisa
que tu rostro me declama.

RENDEZVOUS

Eduardo Mitre

Heavens and centuries
before now,
we had already come
to this morning's light.
You, by a rosary
of pigeons miraculously
chained together. I,
by a branch
of falcons,
nostalgic.
We had already come.
The stone had already come
to be a cornerstone,
the cotton
to be your skirt.
That's the way it is, my love,
that's the way it is,
and even so,
it does not save us. It does not
save us from tomorrow.
Nor does your smile,
proclaiming its face to me,
save us.

Eduardo Mitre

Espejo de miradas
en que nunca me repito

Parabola incesante
Red de ritos

Ella se desnuda
de modos tan distintos

Me faltará vida
para probar todos sus vinos.

POEM 2

Eduardo Mitre

Mirror of glances
where I never repeat myself

Unending parabolas
Net of ritual

She disrobes
in such different ways

There's not enough life
to taste all of her wines.

CARTA

Eduardo Mitre

Se lo dije una vez y para siempre.
Desde el año mutilado de los meses.
Desde los brazos abiertos del puente.
Desde Juan sin trabajo ni casa
y Milena sin pretendiente.
Desde la cara blanca y la cara negra
que muchos blancos y negros no tienen.
Desde esa mujer que, en la esquina infrecuente,
la noche erige como un templo sin fieles.
Desde las limpias estrellas que acaso
no son tan felices como parecen.
Desde la tierra y su sangrienta suerte,
indirectamente se lo dije
como si comentará con los peces:

¡Dichoso el mar! que es uno y como él quiere.

LETTER

Eduardo Mitre

I've told you once and for all
from the year mutilated from the months
from the bridge's gaping arms
from Juan, homeless and without work,
and Milena with no prospects.
From the white face to the black face
that most blacks and whites have neither of.
From that woman down on the corner,
whom the night sets up like a temple without worshippers.
From the immaculate stars perhaps
not so happy as they seem to be.
From the earth and its destiny, bleeding,
indirectly I've told it to all of you,
as if I were talking to the fish:

Blessed is the sea! He has everything the way he wants it.

OLVIDO Y PIEDRA

Eduardo Mitre

El viento deja la cordillera.
Con voz de trueno llama al agua,
pero no hay nubes: solo armas
y sangre. Olvido y piedra.
Solo, sin rostro, a tientas
por una cadena larga—terca—
de matanzas y de lágrimas
en vano busco el tuyo, tierra.
El viento entra: aspero abrazo
apaga mis ojos y la lampara.
Arido, el recuerdo de aquel mar
bate olas de sed en mi garganta.

OBLIVION AND STONE

Eduardo Mitre

The wind leaves the cordillera.
With a thunder-voice it calls to the water,
but there are no clouds: only weapons
and blood. Oblivion and stone.
Alone, with no face, groping
down a long, hard chain
of butchery and tears,
Land, I look for your face.
The wind comes in: its harsh embrace
puts out my eyes and the lamp.
Acrid, the memory of that sea
beats waves of thirst in my throat.

AÑORANZA

Eduardo Mitre

Si el recuerdo fuera una ciudad
y no una estátua
y la ausencia una carta
y no una espalda
y esta noche aquella mañana
y Amsterdam Cochabamba
y este cuarto aquella calle
y esta sombra aquellos árboles
y este nombre aquella cara
y esta lámpara aquella mirada
y aquella boca esta página
y aquel silencio estas palabras.

LONGING

Eduardo Mitre

If only memory were a city
and not a statue
if absence a letter
and not a back
if tonight were that morning
and Amsterdam Cochabamba
if this room were that street
and this shadow those trees
if this name were that face
and this lamp that glance
if that mouth were this page
and that silence these words.

YABA ALBERTO

Eduardo Mitre

Rage, rage against the dying of the light.
—DYLAN THOMAS

I

Entro en el bar forastero
distante.
Pido una cerveza
y espero. Al fin
te veo llegar
delgado y lento
como eras
como siempre serás.

Vacilante
de la puerta miras:
me reconoces:
decienden
los halcones
de tus cejas.
Pido otra cerveza.

Ya a mi lado, pruebas
un sorbo que te sabe extrano.
Luego hojeas los diarios que traias
bajo el brazo
hasta dar
con la página huérfana
donde el encuentro
se borra
y la soledad me rodea.

YABA ALBERTO

Eduardo Mitre

Rage, rage against the dying of the light.
—DYLAN THOMAS

I

Somewhere far away
I go into a strange bar.
I order a beer
and wait. Finally
I see you come in
thin and slow moving
like you used to be
and always will be.

You pause at the door
looking in,
you recognize me,
the hawks
of your eyebrows
relax.
I order another beer.

Beside me now, you take a sip;
it tastes strange to you.
Then you leaf through the newspaper
you had under your arm
till you come
to the orphan page
where our meeting
begins to blur
and solitude surrounds me once again.

II

Entonces comprendo
(y es inutil el llanto, el grito,
la rebeldia):
te has muerto
y no hay mas remedio
que cambiar
el curso del poema
rumbo a tu ausencia
definitiva.

Oh yaba Alberto,
mi semen, my semilla,
mi melancólico, mi sibarita,
mi siervo, mi califa,

mi Marco Aurelio,
mi Lezama Lima
mi Coran, mi Biblia,
mi Labruna, mi Gardel,
dime:
        ahora
            ¿Cómo
volver a la casa?

¿Sentarse a la mesa
con qué cara
con qué ganas?

¿Cómo ir al Prado, yaba,
y jugar la partida
si ya tu muerte nos hizo
generala dormida?

II

Then it sinks in
(and it's no good to cry or yell
or start a row):
you have died
and all I can do
is change
the course of the poem
in the direction of your definitive
absence.

Oh Yaba Alberto,
my semen, my seed,
my melancholy one, my sybarite,
my servant, my caliph,

my Marcus Aurelius,
my Lezama Lima,
my Koran, my Bible,
my Labruna, my Gardel,
tell me
    now:
        How
can I go home?

How can I sit down at the table?
With what face?
To what purpose?

How can I go to the Prado, Yaba,
and pick up dice
if your death cleaned us out
by rolling high?

III

No,
no me pregunto, yaba,
que haces allí, tan tejos,
tan lontananza.
De seguro sequir discutiendo
con el abuelo y don Said

sobre el comercio de lanas,
la espantosa alzar del dólar,
la miseria, el coraje del pueblo,
los militares funestos,
la matanza de palestinos,
la dispersion de tus hijos,
el viaje a Granada que nunca hicimos,
el sabor del duranzno este enero,
los versos que estoy escribiendo,
en fin—así de concretos
son nuestros muertos—
sobre todo los que toca
gozoso vivir
que es el nuestro.

III

   No,
I'm not wondering, Yaba,
what you're doing there
way up yonder.
I'll bet any money you're still arguing
with Grandpa and Don Said

about the wool business,
the terrible hike in the dollar,
squalor, the courage of the people,
military creeps,
the slaughter of Palestinians,
how the children have scattered,
the trip to Granada we never took,
how peaches taste this summer,
the poems I'm writing;
in short, our deaths
are this concrete—
above all, those that touch
the pain and pleasure
of our living.

IV

       Sí
he de volver a la casa,
a tu cuarto, a tu espejo,
a la luz del patio
lleno de tu silencio.
Y a las tardes del Prado
a oirte en los dados
cargados de tu recuerdo.

Pero antes, dime, yaba Alberto:
¿Qué buscabas con tus ojos
secretamente ebrios
de nostalgia?

  ¿El camello imposible
en el país de la llama?
¿Rodeado de montañas
el desierto y la luna
de los origenes?

IV

      Yes,
I have to go back home,
to your room, to your mirror,
to the light on the patio
filled with your silence.
And to afternoons at the Prado
where your memory rattles in my ear
like a pair of loaded dice.

But first, tell me, Yaba Alberto,
What were you looking for
with your eyes secretly drunk
with nostalgia?

  The impossible camel
in the land of the llama?
Surrounded by mountains,
were you seeking the desert and the moon
of beginnings?

EL TORO

Nicomedes Suárez Araúz

Enfrentándonos
con su calavera de yeso diurno
y sus cuernos de mechas grises
el toro se para
nos mira
con ramales oscuros en el ceño
y llamas en los ojos

y por un instante
adquiere la architechtura total del día

antes de desaparecer en los pajonales

THE BULL

Nicomedes Suárez Araúz

Facing us
with his plaster skull
his horns, gray fuses
the bull stands
looks at us
dark bristles on his brow
and flames in his eyes

and for an instant
he takes on the total architecture of the day

before he darts away into the stalls

LAS CARAS INTERIORES

Nicomedes Suárez Araúz

Tejo mis raíces de humus
cerca al fuego
mis manos
arrugado pan y cobre

caen los petalos de mis parpados

los pechos son mangos secos

¡Qué largo el rotar de semilla a semilla!

¿Qué camino sin fin nos mira sin ser visto?

Ciervos de imágenes
saltan de nuestros ojos viejos
al ojo nuevo
        (Equivocados frentes de agua
        chocan en la dura oscuridad infinita
        y nos reconocemos . . .)
Sangra el limón cortado
de la madrugada

alisa los huesos mentales
siglos de polvo de la noche
lavados
solo el cabello antiguo
en los antiguos limites

dentro de la puertas
sigilosos fósforos acechan

y de pronto se incendia
la forma de la mano
y pulsan cantos

INTERIOR FACES

Nicomedes Suárez Araúz

I knit my roots of vegetable mold
close to the fire
my hands
wrinkled bread and copper

the petals of my eyelids fall

The breasts are dry mangos

How long the cycle from seeding to seeding!

What road without end watches us unseen?

Imaginary deer
leap from our old eyes
to the new eye
        (Misguided foreheads of water
        crash into one another in the hard, infinite darkness
        and we recognize each other . . .)
The lemon cut
from the dawn bleeds

It polishes the metaphysical bones
centuries of night's dust,
washed
alone is the ancient head
in ancient boundaries

within the doors
sly matches lurk

and suddenly the form
of a hand catches fire
and songs of body gestures

de ademanes

      (lentamente nuestros
      dientes de luz
      muerden las húmedas
      entranas de la tierra
      caen las cascaras mentales
      y surgimos a ciudades verdes)

Lentamente reconocemos las calles
      nosotros vivimos
      él vive
      tú vives
      yo vivo
      por el cañaveral
      y la maleza
      con gruñidos
      por el pasto
      con siseo y relámpago
      por el agua
      con un llamear de aletas
      y de cola

      y por el aire
      por el aire
      por el aire amarillo
      las alas de nuestras caras
      interiores
      vuelan
      hasta donde
      arden las palabras
      y el silencio (sin labios)

      Aquí nace la poesía.

throb

        (Slowly
        our teeth of light
        bite the watery
        bowels of the earth
        metaphysical husks drop off
        and we surge to green cities)
Slowly we recognize streets
        we live
        he lives
        you live
        I live
        for the cane field
        and the underbrush
        with grunts
        and for the grass
        with hissing and lightning
        and for the water
        ablaze with fins
        and tails

        and for the air
        for the air
        for the yellow air
        the wings
        of our interior faces
        fly up
        to where words
        are burning
        and the (lipless) silence

        Here poetry is born.

CHAPARRÓN

Nicomedes Suárez Araúz

Cabalgamos

y una sombra verde
se nos pega a la espalda

las primeras gotas
chocan contra la geometría de la tarde
y la disuelven

detrás de las miradas
el chaparrón pace
con su largo pelo de animal salvaje

TROPICAL SHOWER

Nicomedes Suárez Araúz

We are riding

and a green shade
fastens to our backs

the first drops beat
against the geometry of the afternoon
and dissolve it

behind our eyes
the shower is grazing
with its shaggy, wild animal coat

PATOS EN LA LAGUNA DEL CARMEN

Nicomedes Suárez Araúz

a Winston

El chillido blanco de los patos
en el crepúsculo
siembra zanjas en el cielo
y hace palidecer al pasto.

La laguna desesperada
trata de atrapar sus vuelos
pero ellos, organismos
de sombra, reconocen
el crujir de los ojos del cazador.

DUCKS IN THE LAGOON AT EL CARMEN

Nicomedes Suárez Araúz

to Winston

The white shrieking of ducks
in the twilight
furrows the sky
and whitens the grass.

Desperately, the lagoon
tries to capture their flight
but they, organisms of shadow,
know and recognize
the creak of the eyes of the hunter.

CABALLO BLANCO

Nicomedes Suárez Araúz

Entre sombras de árboles
baja al arroyo
un caballo blanco.

Las carnes trémulas del verde
vibran de luto ajeno
sólo un pueril brillo de luna
rubrica sus caras.

El arroyo envuelve al caballo
con su gasa líquida
y todo cae en la indolencia
de un solo plano,

caballo agua y ramales
se sorben unos a otros.

WHITE HORSE

Nicomedes Suárez Araúz

Among the shadows of the trees
down to the creek bank
goes a white horse.

The trembling flesh of the foliage
shivers with borrowed mourning,
only an infantile light from the moon
outlines the faces of the leaves.

The stream enfolds the horse
with its liquid vapor
and everything falls into the indolence
of a single plane—

horse, foliage, and water
drink one another.

DESDE EL JARDÍN DEL MORADOR

Blanca Wiethüchter

Cuando desnuda, mi alma
se mostró
dividida
taciturna y mediosa
dejé la montaña y
me fui a vivir entre los árboles
    —invulnerables—pensé
al verlos en las avenidas
hermosas y sencillos.

La ciudad de los árboles esperados
era verde
con bandera verde
y ángeles—creo—tambien verdes.

Tal vez—me dije—podría en esta ciudad
despertar la memoria
de aquel lugar claro y luminoso
    oculto
en otra
    antigua
     vida.

El primer día
    olvidé la impaciencia
—era invierno.
Los árboles se iluminaban del puro florecer
y los pájaros estuvieron a punto
        de revelarme un secreto.
Hubo mariposas y por la noche lechuzas.

El día siguiente
    temblorosa
me sorprendió ver

FROM WITHIN THE DWELLER'S GARDEN

Blanca Wiethüchter

Naked, my soul
showed itself
divided
fearful and subdued.
I left the mountain
and went to live among the trees
        —they're invulnerable—I thought
having seen them so simple and beautiful
in the avenues.

The city of waiting trees
was green
with green banners
and with angels—I'm quite sure—also green.

Perhaps—I told myself—it might be possible in this city
to awaken memory
from some clear luminous place
        hidden now
in some other
        ancient
        life.

The first day
        I lost the memory of impatience
—it was winter.
The trees were lit up in pure blossom
and birds were on the brink
                        of revealing their secrets.
There were butterflies, moths, owls in the night.

The next day
        trembling,
I was surprised to see

en la inmensidad azul que resucitaba
un hermoso saludo
era como si un angel mío
      —exhausto
me invitará a entrar en otro sueño.

Esto es morada de reyes
—me dije—al tercer día.
      ¿Podrá ser la mía?

in the immenseness, a blue that breathed
a beautiful greeting,
it was as if one of my weary angels
     —exhausted
were inviting me to enter another dream.

This is a dwelling for kings
—I told myself—on the third day.
     Could it be for me?

Blanca Wiethüchter

Mediodía:
transparentes en el azul
     se abrazan sin reproche:
la hora de la angustia
el vuelo de la ley:
voraz el águila—erizado el reptil.

4

Blanca Wiethüchter

Midday:
transparent in the azure blue
     they embrace without reproach.
The hour of anguish,
the flight of the law:
voracious eagle—bristling reptile.

5

Blanca Wiethüchter

Invisible es el tigre
y no es sólo un decir.
Errante,
entre el mundo de los vivos
y el mundo de los muertos
sueña
con el bosque
en su sangre.

5

Blanca Wiethüchter

Invisible is the tiger
and it's not a mere phrase.
Nomadically wandering,
between the world of the living
and the world of the dead,
he dreams
of the forest
in his blood.

6

Blanca Wiethüchter

Una palmera
memoriza
la voz del viento:
lomas blancas
    lomas de arena
presagiando el desierto.

El verde no vuelve del sol.
El sol no devuelve el verde.

camino agobiada.

(Ahora,
ahora mismo
    por el hombre
    llora la madera.)

6

Blanca Wiethüchter

A palm tree
memorizes
the voice of the wind:
white hills
    hills of sand
predicting the omen of a desert.

        The green does not come back from the sun.
        The sun does not give back the green.

        Head bowed, I walk, oppressed.

        (Now,
        at this very moment
           the wood weeps
        for Man.)

SOLO

Elias Serrano Pantoja

Estoy solo como quise estarlo
Como la muerte sin funeral

Solo como el olvido que pudre la inconciencia
Como la tristeza que quema una lagrima

Veo la gente como un grito dormido
En la redondez de la nada
Como la ventana que no cuaja la luz
Como la iglesia apagada en rezos
Estar solo
Estar solo es mirarse con los ojos del alma
Estar solo es amar las cenizas
Para arder al rescoldo
Estar solo es llenarse de sombras
Para parir una flor
Estoy solo como quise estarlo.

ALONE

Elias Serrano Pantoja

I am alone as I wanted to be
Like a death without a funeral

Alone like the oblivion that rots the unconsciousness
Like the sadness that burns tears

I see all the people like a sleeping scream
In the rotundity of nothingness
Like a window that can't let in light
Like a cathedral out of prayers
To be alone
To be alone is to look at oneself through the eyes of the soul
To be alone is to love ashes
To burn to cinders
To be alone is to fill up with shadow
So a flower can be born
I am alone as I wanted.

EL ULTIMO QUIJOTE

Elias Serrano Pantoja

Yo no imprimo carácteres sobre lapida,
recojo la salmodia de mis rondas interiores
para alivar mi niebla con sus sones.

Por la armargura de mis palabras mendigas,
voy viajando en góndolas de viento
para eximirme de los sueños de la infancia.

La inerte cintura de las cruces
agita la bandera inerme de una brisa
forjada en el tormento del adiós.

De nada sirve el llanto aislado
en trevesia ineficaz contra la inercia.
Es la masa de fanáticos beodos
que escribe glorias
con la mayuscula invención de carcajadas.

Indulgencia pido para mi hambre
de inmersión en la quietud;
libertad para mi ingravida nostalgia.
Quiero que las luces para mi manantial
de niebla irreprimible.

Soy isleno combatiendo en soledad.
Soy roca que se rompe contra el mar
aunque lo ignore el ojo blanco de la luna.
Soy la primicia del último Quijote
para el latigazo de mi suerte.

THE LAST QUIXOTE

Elias Serrano Pantoja

I don't scribble figures on slate,
I pick up the melodious song of my interior serenades
to lighten the weight of my cloud with its sounds.

Through the bitterness of my beggar words,
I go traveling in gondolas of wind
to free myself from the dreams of infancy.

The inert belt of crosses
ruffles the enormous flag of a breeze
forged in the torment of a farewell.

The isolated howl is good for nothing
in crosswinds useless against inertia.
It is the mass of fanatic drunkards
inscribing glories
with the capital invention of cackling laughter.

I ask indulgence for my hunger,
for immersion in quietude,
the freedom of a weightless nostalgia.
I want lights for my fountain
of irrepressible cloud.

I'm an islander combating the loneliness.
I'm a rock that breaks against the sea.
Though the moon's white eye is ignorant of it,
I'm the novelty of the last Quixote
for the scourge of my destiny.

ALBORADA RUSTICA

Elias Serrano Pantoja

El letargo matinal de las llanuras
sacude la tierra ensimismada,
y rompe bruscamente
el rostro repentino del sol.

Las mujeres de mi pueblo oculto
repican su lenguaje de tinajas aguateras
en su vaiven caminante de llamaradas.
Parece que sus cuerpos dibujaran liras.
Y sus pies desnudos
hurgaran la concupiscente tierra.

Los hisopos de hierba
despiertan a su paso
en la vereda
de los senderos de relampagos,
y desgranan las estrellas sel rocio.
Las chicharras desgranan su arido lamento,
y nace la vida,
                    y nace la luz.
Revienta la lucha
por un pedazo de pan
                    y de miseria.

RUSTIC DAYBREAK

Elias Serrano Pantoja

The lazy morningsong of the prairie
shakes the distracted earth
and harshly breaks
the reptilian face of the sun.

The women of my hidden village
peal out their earthy language
in their flurry of comings and goings.
Their bodies seem to draw lines.
Their naked feet
plow through the concupiscent earth.

The hyssop grasses
wake at their passing
in the lane
of the lightning paths,
shaking the stars out of the dew.
The cicadas scatter their dry wails
and life is born,
              light is born.
The struggle is boiling up
for a bit of bread
              and misery.

PASEO EQUINOCCIAL

Luis Andrade Sanjines

Encuéntrome estremecido entre dos muros.
Los ojos rellenos de desvelo.
El párpado nocturno cae lento
como una torre de bruces contra el suelo.
Para mirarme dentro no uso mi esqueleto.
Asómome al fondo desnudas mis pupilas.
Abismo, abismo oscuro lámpara de sombras.
Precipítome sin voz al mediodía
que cruza cenital mi desaliento.
Allí está ausente mi pena visceral,
                    mi ancha pena.
Es un río ansioso y estirado.
Peces de luz caen sobre mi frente.
Mi mano hace señales angustiadas.
Adiós, adiós.
Hasta que otra vez tenga que irme.
El viento se anuda a mi destino
como mudo nudo marinero
de gruesa soga fría y casual recuento.
Entro al banquete de los desesperados
vestido de silencios,
con pie izquierdo y brazos enlutados.
Nadie repara en mí,
en el temblor latiente de mis poros.
Lluevo sobre el paisaje con mi canto.

EQUINOCTIAL STROLL

Luis Andrade Sanjines

I find myself trembling between two walls.
My eyes overflow with keeping watch.
The nocturnal eyelid falls slowly
like a tower headlong against the ground.
To look within myself I don't use my skeleton.
I go down into the depths with my naked pupils.
Abyss, dark abyss, lamp of shadows.
I throw myself down, voiceless to the noontime
that crosses the zenith of my despair.
My visceral pain is absent there,
                    my vast pain.
It is an anxious, stretched out river.
Fish of light fall on my forehead.
My hand makes anguished signals.
Good-bye, good-bye.
Till I have to leave again.
The wind knots itself to my destiny
like a mute sailor's knot
of thick, cold rope and casual inventory.
I go into the banquet of the desperate,
dressed in silences,
with my left foot and my arms in mourning.
No one notices me,
the pulsing shudder of my pores.
I rain down on the landscape with my song.

AMOR POLÍTICO

Luis Andrade Sanjines

La revolución, muchacha
tiene como tú senos frutales,
muslos maduros y firmes
caderas frescas y dulces,
sexo oscuro y caliente.

Por eso,
cada vez que te miro a los ojos
la recuerdo,
y la persigo igual que a tí
para poseerla y amarla
como a tí te poseo y te amo:
con locura.

POLITICAL LOVE

Luis Andrade Sanjines

The revolution, lady,
has, like you, fruitful breasts,
thighs, mature and firm,
hips, fresh and sweet,
sex, hot and dark.

Because of that,
each time I look into your eyes
I remember it,
I pursue it as I do you,
to love it and possess it
as I love and possess you:
with madness.

PALABRA

Luis Andrade Sanjines

desde fuera
            del tiempo
te veo venir
extrañamente vestida de pasiones
y solemne   te acercas
a mis sueños   desnudándote

      Palabra en el caos
     p
       r
         e
           c
             i
               p
                 i
                   t
                     a
      r
    o   m
  tu f   a
    y tu silencio
el espacioes un árbol
que capta
bajo el fuego   frío
regresando de pronto

                          piedras
                    las
               de
           alto
        lo
  desde

WORD

Luis Andrade Sanjines

from outside
                of time
I see you come
strangely dressed in passions
and solemn   you approach
my dreams   stripping yourself nude

      Word in the chaos
       L
          a
             u
                n
                    c
                  h
                e
                  s

           r
        o   m
your f
      and your silence
space   is a tree
that captivates
under the cold   fire
returning suddenly

                    stones
               the
            of
      height
    the
from

                miro tu imagen   y despierto
                   pensando en el humo
                          dentro
                    soy un río
                      tenue red   sereno movimiento
    la noche es mujer   cuerpo y
                      sal   to
                   a lo lejos   de la luz presente
             te conjuro   y armado de evidencias
         beso tu boca honda   toco tu mano
            tu piel de roca   ardiendo
                  tu voz   en la sombra
                             es música

                   en el viento

          Decir es un acto   para mover el alma

          y tu Palabra   puedes
                puñal y/o arado
                     al
mismo

                   tiempo.

I look at your image   and I awake
            thinking of the smoke
                    inside
        I am a river
            tenuous net   serene movement
    the night is woman   body and
                I   jump
    from the far distance   to the present light
        I conjure you   and armed with evidence
    I kiss your deep mouth   I touch your hand
        your skin of burning   rock
            your voice   in the shadow
                    is music

            in the wind

    Saying is an act   to move the soul

        and you, Word   can
                dagger and/or plow
                    at the
same

                    time . . .

Freddy Estremadoiro Romero

Los sueños serán sueños
mientras vivan
Gracias por recordarme
en la espera de los miedos
nunca escritos
en caminos distantes
promesas de nieve
gotas perdidas
en calles lluviosas
el amor compartido.
Sombras de ensueños.

Freddy Estremadoiro Romero

Dreams will be dreams
while they live
Thank you for reminding me
of the hope of fears
never written
of distant roads
promises of snow
lost drops
in rainy streets
of love shared.
Fantasy shadows.

Freddy Estremadoiro Romero

Muchachuela mimosa vestida de nombres
háblame de tus tropezones
de tu cara sin lavar mirando a los mil
que te casas y no te sacas porque no te gustan

los botones dorados
háblame mas pelada alborotilla de tus
          caderas para procrear
si tienes vergüenza desnudaré sólo el alma
de tu vestido mojado colgando su etiqueta
          china
cuanto cambian tus trajes es sólo una
          pregunta
para bailar con esa mímica que aún
          te queda en el color

Freddy Estremadoiro Romero

Spoiled little girl dressed in names
speak to me of your blunders
of your unwashed face looking at the thousand
may you marry and may you not go out because you don't like

gold-plated buttons
speak to me some more, naked troublemaker, of your
      hips made for childbearing
if you're ashamed I'll strip only your soul
from your damp dress, hanging with its label
      made in China
How many times you change clothes is only
      a question
to dance with that imitation that still
      has your same color

Freddy Estremadoiro Romero

Siento haberte esperado
con toda la carga
que inventé
pero ahora que te mueres
y los gorriones
crean nuevos juegos
para tu ausencia
presiento una duda
que jamás será una flor

Freddy Estremadoiro Romero

I feel I've waited for you
with all the baggage
that I've invented
but now that you're dying
and the seagulls
invent new games
for your absence
I foresee a doubt
that will never be a flower

LA JUSTICIA

Amilkar Jaldín

Perseguir el grito.
No el nuestro,
el de los otros;
desde la mancha
roja
a la mortaja
blanca.
Y al final encontrarnos
con la Dama
sin balanza
golpeando a ciegas
con su espada
rota.

JUSTICE

Amilkar Jaldín

To follow the scream.
Not ours,
the others';
from the red
stain
to the white
shroud.
And finally we find ourselves
with the Lady
but without the balance
striking blind blows
with her broken
sword.

DE ESTA VIDA

Amilkar Jaldín

El benemerito,
cara al cielo,
indiferente al abrazo
y a los ruegos,
tan firme como nunca,
mas que en el chaco,
ni se percatara
que la banda
lo acompanara solo dos cuadras,
ni que la cura,
en su presencia,
le dedico la misa
a otro difunto.

FROM THIS LIFE

Amilkar Jaldín

The worthy one,
face to the sky,
indifferent to embraces
and to pleading,
more adamant than ever,
more than in the *chaco,*
is not even aware
that the band
will go only two blocks
nor that the priest
in his presence
has dedicated the mass
to the wrong body.

GRITO ORIENTAL

Alejandro Mara

Quiero atravesar
los hilos
invertebrados de
la luz

para ser el eslabón
humano
que late
en la gota vegetal
que estalla
en la armoniosa
tempestad de las palmeras.

ORIENTAL SCREAM

Alejandro Mara

I want to
pass through
the spineless threads
of light

to be the human
swivel
that throbs
in the vegetal drop
that bursts
in the harmonious
tempest of the palms.

VIENTRE PROFUNDO

Alejandro Mara

De las aguas del cielo bajaban
los pájaros a la tierra inmensa.
El sol derretía su esperma caliente.
Las palmeras inclinaban sus cuerpos
al vapor espumoso de las arenas.
Y de las oscuras hilanderias del tiempo
tu voz era una madera quemada.
Giró en un movimiento la rueda del sol
y seres hambrientos
emergieron de pronto
de tu vientre profundo.

DEEP WOMB

Alejandro Mara

From the waters of heaven the birds
came down to the vast earth.
The sun squandered his hot sperm.
The palm trees leaned their bodies
toward the foaming vapor of the sands.
And out of time's dark spinning wheels
came your voice of burned wood.
The wheel of the sun whirled in movement
and hungry beings
suddenly emerged
from your deep womb.

INSTANTE MERIDIONAL

Alejandro Mara

Cuando las aguas suban al aire
y la luz inmortal
toque mis hombros desnudos
Dame a mí
el mediodía

Cuando la lluvia cese de golpear los tejados
y el sol salga a vencer el palido día
depositando cal y fuego
sobre las cigarras y las raices
Dame a mí
el mediodía

Cuando esté ausente,
lejos de tus manos
y venga la tristeza
a robarme los secretos de la espuma
largamente conquistado
En mi última hora
en mi último salto desesperado
Dame
el mediodía
el sonoro y ardiente mediodía

MERIDIAN INSTANT

Alejandro Mara

When the waters have mounted to the air
and immortal light
touches my naked shoulders
Give me
the noon.

When the rain has ceased to beat on the rooftops
and the sun comes out to vanquish the pallid day
sending out fire and brimstone
over the locusts and the roots
Give me
the noon.

When I am absent
far from your hands
and sadness comes
to rob from me the secrets of the seafoam,
long since conquered
in my last hour,
in my last desperate leap
Give me the noon
the resonant
and burning noon.

LARGO DESEO HUMEDO

Alejandro Mara

Cuando las espumas humedezcan
los túneles secos del tiempo
y las aguas cansadas, las harinas
los telares y los machetes
lleguen definitivamente a su destino único
Yo quiero una vasija, una vertebra humana
un cuerpo cargando pesadas mazorcas derrotadas,
un azadón enterrado en la tierra mas dura
Quiero una cigarra veloz, una palmera vencedora
unas manos que sujeten el vientre dulce
de las naranjas
y se levanten bruscamente buscando
pozos oscuros, células desamparadas
tristes superfícies donde se acumula la
miseria y el sufrimiento
Yo quiero unos ojos ardientes, decididamente ardientes
unos dientes que muerdan, trituren
y salgan dando gritos
cuando nos destruyan la razón, la región y los zapatos
Yo junto a la arena callo y espero largamente,
una lluvia fecunda, un aserradero, y una esperanza
como un puñado de arroz repartido
o una tela recién lavada.

LONG DAMP DESIRE

Alejandro Mara

When the vapors moisten
the dry tunnels of time
and the tired waters, the grains of meal,
the textile mills and the machetes
finally reach their only destiny
I want a vessel, a human spine
a body carrying heavy, broken spindles
a hoe, buried in the hard earth
I want a swift cicada, a conquering palm tree
hands that clutch the sweet belly
of the orange
and rise up brusquely, looking for
dark ponds, deserted cells
sad surfaces where misery
and suffering are growing.
I want eyes, burning, decidedly burning
teeth that bite, that crush and pulverize
and go out screaming
when they destroy our reason, our territory and our shoes
Near the sand I remain quiet, patient
like a handful of chaffed grain
or a fabric freshly washed,
waiting for a sawmill, a hope, a fertile rain.

LAMENTO INÚTIL

Alejandro Mara

No quiero seguir siendo una gota inútil.
Una tutuma partida por dentro.
Un tatú cavando la tierra.
Ay no quiero tanta adversidad para mi vida
hallarme abandonado en el medio lia tripulado de silencio
Como una estatua cerrada y sin altura.

Inclino mi cabeza a la base humeda de la arena
para mirarte
pero solo veo tus ojos martillados
tus manos gastadas por el borde redondo de las cucharas
y tu sexo intacto entre las piernas
como una corriente de agua muerta.
Por eso
cuando subo mi rostro al centro luminoso del día,
no solo busco tus manos
o pedazos de tu voz destituida,
sino tambien arrastro angustias, viejas tristezas endurecida.

Yo no sé donde se halla la perpetuidad del tiempo
ni sé quien le puso belleza a la gota de rocio
que moja el chirimoyo,
lo cierto,
es que me encuentro a tu lado
húmedo de lágrimas
abordando horas esteriles, inalterables.
Y cuando regreso del fondo de la tarde lejana
cansado,
desamparado de ilusiones
Y miro las frazadas desordenadas de tu cama
nuestro barrio con sus postes de luz y pozos de agua lenta
Ay muchas veces siento
un rencor caliente en mi pecho
por todas esas cosas que son difíciles de cambiar.

USELESS LAMENT

Alejandro Mara

I don't want to go on being a useless drop
a hump cut in half from inside
a repetitious digging into the earth.
Oh, I'm tired of so much adversity in my life
finding myself abandoned at noon, driven by silence
like a locked up statue without stature.

I lower my head to the damp base of the sand
to look at you
but I see only your tormented eyes
your hands wasted on the rounded rims of spoons
your sex, intact between your legs
like a current of dead water.
Because of that
when I lift my face to the luminous center of the day,
not only do I search for your hands
or pieces of your destitute voice,
but also I pull up anguish: old, hardened sadnesses.

I don't know wherein lies the constancy of time.
I don't know who put beauty into the dewdrops
that wet the crab apples.
The only certainty
is that I am here by your side
drenched with tears
taking on sterile, unalterable hours.
And when I return from the depths of the far afternoon
fatigued
bereft of illusions
and I look at the rumpled blankets of your bed
our barrio with its lamp posts and its stagnant ponds.
Oh, often I feel
a burning rancor in my breast
for all those things so difficult to change

Por todo lo que tenemos que aceptar
con resignación y orgullo
y por lo impuro y violento que resulta vivir.

Arrimate a las sombras impostergables de los grandes mangales
junto a mi ser demolido
para que pueda alcanzar tus hombros desnudos
y sentir en la punta de mi boca
los nervios dulces de tus senos
que de pronto se levantan
como flores erguidas de sangre
como símbolos de una vida articula la de esfuerzos
y largas resistencias.

Hunde en mí tus aguas cansadas
Y llora con tus lágrimas de acero derretido
que yo también lloro
cuando salgo a buscar la vida
con sus almahadas sucias
y alambres oxizadas de ropa vieja.

Quiero desatar la tela que oprime el musculo de la mariposa.
Romper el instrumento que calla tu conciencia.
Hallar nuevos fuegos, forjar nuevos simbolos liberadores.
Ser una enredadera que trepa por tu cuerpo moreno.

Busco habitar dentro de tus hojos tenaces
para que el tiempo no me destruya
con su vacio decididamente material.

for all that we have to accept
with pride and resignation
and for the impurities and violence brought on by living.

Snuggle up to the inevitable shadows of the great mangos
here, next to my demolished self
where I can touch your bare shoulders
and feel against my mouth
the sweet sinews of your breasts
which suddenly bloom
like flowers swelled with blood
symbols of life uttered with forced effort
and long resistance.

Submerge in me your tired waters
and cry with your tears of melted steel
which I also cry
as I go out looking for life
with its dirty cushions
and rusted threads of old clothes.

I want to unravel the fabric that presses on the muscles of the butterfly
to break the instrument that quiets your consciousness
to find new fires, forge new, free symbols
to be a net that drapes over your dark body.

I look for habitation within your tenacious eyes
so that time need not destroy me
infinitely material void.

POEMAS

Rubén Vargas

Fluyen
sin tiempo
y
crecen
con el ritmo
de su propio silencio

Los cuerpos
llenan la noche

▪ ▪ ▪

el perfil
de la noche
sorprende
tu espalda

y
eres espejo
de otra desnudez
retorna
mi cuerpo
desnudo

▪ ▪ ▪

no elijes   no elijo
    ni la noche
    ni los astros
    ni el relámpago
    que nos une
            y
    nos separa
    nada es nuestro
elijo   elijes
    el vertigo
    que nos disuelve

POEMS

Rubén Vargas

They flow
without time
and grow
in the rhythm
of their own
silence

The bodies
that fill the night

▪ ▪ ▪

The profile
of night
surprises
your back

and you
are a mirror
from another
nudeness
my nude body
turns

▪ ▪ ▪

You don't choose   I don't choose
   the night
   nor the stars
   nor the lightning
   that unites us
      and
   separates us
   nothing is ours
I choose   you choose
   the vertigo
   that dissolves us

tus hombros
quiebran
el tallo
de la noche
desconcertadas aves
tus ropas
anidan en el piso

La tierra que hierre
la curvatura de tus senos
tus senos
que dibujan
este arco de luz

lejana lluvia
lluvia

lejana
llueve

tu cabellera sin fin

■ ■ ■

Vienes de la luz
y te despojas

porque el amor
no admite sino
la forma del desorden

vienes de la ciudad
y la ahuyentas

eres
tu cuerpo
y la alta noche
hundida en tu costado

■ ■ ■

your shoulders
break
the stalk
of the night
your clothes
flustered birds
flung out on the floor

The earth that wounds
the curvature of your breasts
your breasts
that sketch
an arc of light

far-off rain
rain

faraway
it's raining

your endless flowing hair

■　■　■

You come from out of the light
and you undress

because love
admits only
the form of disorder

you come from out of the city
and you frighten it

you are
your body
and the tall night
buried in your rib

■　■　■

sólo
una línea
nos separa del mundo

tu piel

■　■　■

tu cuerpo
voracidad/veracidad
me ata a la tierra

el alba
trae tu nombre
dormido
mi cuerpo

ignora la luz
dueña
de
la noche
dispersada

astros
redimidos
orillan
tu cuerpo

playa
de silencios

■　■　■

Only
a line
separates us from the world

your skin

■ ■ ■

your body
voracity/veracity
ties me to the earth

the dawn
brings your name
sleeping
my body

knows
nothing
of the light
mistress
of the scattered night

The stars
redeemed
trim
your body

beach
of quietness

■ ■ ■

DE VECINIDADES, TRES POSTALES

Viviana Limpias Chavez

I. La muerte, mi vecina,
me golpeó la puerta al mediodía
venía a pedirme
"una tazita de arrepentimiento"
y una pizca
"solo una pizca"
de cobardía.
—Vuelve mañana—le dije.
Y esa noche me mudé.

II. La muerte, mi vecina
me descubrió una tarde
con los ojos vendados,
cubierta de frazadas
que olían
a cuerpos sucios y aterrados.
No la ahuyento ese olor, estoy segura,
porque ese mismo día
llevó a Zulmamariaelenabenjaybraco
que portaban idénticas frazadas.
La muerte cazaba botas militares.

III. La muerte, mi vecina,
hasta ya de que le ande esquivocando,
vendrá descalza un día
a llevarse mis huesos
a un país de lluvias sin futuros.
¡Ojalá que se ahogue en mis cenizas!

THREE POSTCARDS

Viviana Limpias Chavez

I. Death, my neighbor
knocked on the door at noon.
She'd come to ask me
for just a cup of regret
and a pinch
just a pinch
of cowardice.
Come back tomorrow, I said.
And that night I moved.

II. Death, my neighbor
discovered me one afternoon
with blindfolded eyes
and covered with blankets
that stank
of dirty, buried bodies.
She didn't notice the smell, I'm sure
because that same day
she carried off Zulmamariaelenabenjaybraco
who had identical blankets.
The dead woman was wearing combat boots.

III. Death, my neighbor
I've managed to give the slip up until now.
One day she'll sneak up on me barefooted
to carry off my bones
to a land of futureless rains.
May she drown in my ashes!

ALTERNATIVA

Viviana Limpias Chavez

Hicimos el amor y fue conjuro
contra la muerte
que revolteaba
como grotesca mariposa oscura
por sobre nuestro martes desvelado.

Hicimos el amor y se cayeron
todos los frutos amargos de mi cuerpo,
y entonces fue el futuro,
y aquella mariposa,
derrotada,
plegó sus alas,
se durmió mansamente
entre mis piernas
borracha de los jugos de la siembra.

ALTERNATIVE

Viviana Limpias Chavez

We made love and it was a plot
against death
that fluttered around
like a grotesque, dark night-moth
over our watchful Tuesday.

We made love and all
the bitter fruits of my body fell,
and then it was the future,
and that moth,
vanquished,
folded it wings,
slept heavily
between my legs,
drunk on the juices of seedtime.

Antonio Rojas

Para empuñarte contra las sombras
para marcar golpes el camino
entre los escombros,
desde mi nacimiento
fui eligiendo tu arcilla:
no la que duerme a flor de tierra,
no la que añora una cima,
no la que mata una hoja,
hasta encontrarla
la busqué con las uñas
con los dientes
la arranqué del corazón de la tierra,
y elegí el agua
no la que finge ser cielo,
no la que pasa gimiendo,
no la obstinada en el mar,
busqué la pura
la que vibra al contacto con la tierra
Te di la forma de una vasija
y te llené de luz,
cargo contigo
por todos los caminos
para aplacar a los sedientos
que marchan solitarios
a la zaga:
y para los que marchan
adelante,
para todos te llevo, alta como una bandera.
Refresca tambien la garganta
y el corazón de otros
de aquellos que jamás encontraré.

Antonio Rojas

To clutch you against the shadows
To stamp my tracks on the road
through the wreckage
since I was born
I've been selecting your clay:
not the kind that sleeps on the earth's surface,
not the kind that yearns for a hilltop
not the kind that kills leaves,
until I found it
I looked for it with my fingernails
and with my teeth
I pulled it up out of the heart of the earth,
and I chose the water
not the kind that pretends to be the heavens
not the kind that flows by sighing,
not the obstinate kind of the sea,
I looked for the pure
that vibrates at the touch of the earth
I gave you the form of a vessel
and I filled you with light,
I bear you
through all roads
to appease the thirsty
that march alone
behind,
and those that march
in front
for all of them I carry you, high like a banner.
Refresh the throats
and the hearts of others as well,
refresh all those whom I shall never meet.

Antonio Rojas

El grande le pegaba con un látigo;
El pequeño, que estaba atado,
se mordía los labios y no gritaba;
El grande le pegaba, le pegaba y le pegaba.
Cuando se cansó de pegarle,
se fue a tomar una cerveza.
El pequeño se desató como pudo
y buscó una salida.
El grande se levantó con la cerveza
y volvió donde el pequeño.
Cuando el grande abrió la puerta
el pequeño salió corriendo.
Entonces apagué el televisor
para que todo quede oscuro
y el pequeño pueda escapar.

Antonio Rojas

The big one was beating him with a club
The smaller one, tied up,
bit his lip but did not cry out.
The big one beat him and beat him and beat him
When he got tired of beating him
He went off to get a beer.
The smaller one managed to untie himself
and started looking for a way out.
The big one got up with his beer
and came back to the room where the smaller one was.
When the big one opened the door
the smaller one came running out.
That's when I turned off the television
so it would be dark
and the smaller one could get away.

ODA AL MEON

Antonio Rojas

Oh ¡qué sensación!
Orinar en una calle céntrica
sin más ni más.
Todos vuelcan a mirarte
como si fueras Superman
o algo parecido.

Sentir que infringes
una norma
que acabas con ella
cual si fuese un terrón de azúcar
al que le dejes caer agua.

Los que van en auto
te enfocan con sus luces
creyendo que tienes en la mano
una linterna de rayos ultravioleta.

y gozas más aún
cuando estás terminando de orinar
y desde la otra vereda,
una morena te la sacude
con sus pestañas.

ODE TO PEEING

Antonio Rojas

Oh, what a sensation!
To urinate in the open street
no more, no less,
everyone turning their heads to look at you
as if you were a Superman
or something.

To feel yourself infringing
upon a norm—
that you are finishing it
as if it were a barrel of sugar
and you were pouring water into it.

Those going by in cars
would focus their lights on you
wondering if what you had in your hand
was an ultraviolet light.

And your greatest pleasure would be,
when done with urinating,
that from the other sidewalk
a lovely brunette
should bat her eyes at you.

LLEGÓ PAPÁ NOEL

Renzo Gismondi Zumarán

Llegó Papá Noel
Corrí presto a sus brazos,
Sacó una Magnum 45
y me asaltó.

Era todo mi sueldo.
Ahora no tengo Navidad.

FATHER CHRISTMAS CAME

Renzo Gismondi Zumarán

Father Christmas came;
I ran gleefully into his arms.
He smiled at me,
then pulled out a 45 Magnum
and mugged me.

It was my whole paycheck.
Now I don't have Christmas anymore.

Renzo Gismondi Zumarán

Quisiera arrimarme un poquito
a tu corazón
pero . . .

huelen mal tus zapatos.

Renzo Gismondi Zumarán

I longed to draw near
a little closer to your heart
but . . .

your feet stink.

Que miedo escondido trae la noche,
abisman mis pasos en el sendero . . .
La luna, donde escapara la noche
envuelta de miedo no acude.

Rolando Parejas Eguía

What hidden fear the night brings;
my feet sink into the footpath . . .
and where the night would escape,
wrapped in fear, the moon won't come out.

CANTAR

Rolando Parejas Eguía

Cálida soledad el campo
la mañana y la brisa

Lírico son prolongado
naturaleza que trina

Por todas partes vaga
íntima voz de mi dicha

La alegría.

SINGING

Rolando Parejas Eguía

Peppery solitude, the field
the breeze, the morning

lyrical song prolonged,
nature that trills,

everywhere wanders
the intimate voice of my good fortune:

joy.

LA CALLE

Rolando Parejas Eguía

Mar erizado, rugientes olas
—isla calma la morada—
Clamantes crestas de mar, llaman sonoras.

THE STREET

Rolando Parejas Eguía

Bristling sea, rumbling waves
—calm island the dwelling place—
Clamoring crests, they cry out, sonorously calling.

UNA GOTA CAE EN EL SILENCIO

Reymi Ferreira

Una gota cae en el silencio.
Se acumulan los átomos
esperando su turno.

La gota de agua se forma
en segundos y pico,
la gota se forma redonda y translucida.

La gota tiembla como pechos de
mujer
esa gota tremula,
esas gotas que parecen senos,
esa gota que tiembla y se niega a caer.

A DROP FALLS IN THE SILENCE

Reymi Ferreira

A drop is falling in the silence,
all the atoms build up
waiting for their turn.

The water drop is forming
in a matter of seconds,
the drop becomes round and translucid.

The drop trembles like the breasts
of a woman,
that tremulous drop,
those drops like breasts,
that trembling drop that refuses to fall.

DESFLORAMIENTO

Reymi Ferreira

Corre la tarde sin prisa,
suave y débil caricia
su mano en la infinitud de la brisa.

Desnudas y pobres sus nalgas,
caen los bluejeans hasta el suelo,
sus muslos de nacar tiemblan tibios.

Dulzura de agosto,
piel de leche y venado,
sopor de objecciones rendidas.

Un vaho, un vaho como un pájaro
de mal agüero me invade con
un sentimiento de culpa;

mientras solloza, solloza,
sigue sollozando, en mi alma
(esa mujer) sequirá sollozando
eternamente.

—Una vez se deshoja una rosa
ni con cemento se prenden sus hojas—

THE DEFLOWERING

Reymi Ferreira

The afternoon runs without hurry
softly and weakly caressing
her hand in the infiniteness of the breeze.

From her poor nude bottom
the bluejeans fall to the floor,
her mother of pearl flesh trembles warm in my eager hands.

Sweetness of August,
doeskin, milk soft,
drowsiness of protests, surrendering.

A vapor, a vapor like a bird of ill omen
invades me
with a sense of blame

while she sobs and sobs,
keeps sobbing in my soul,
(that woman) will go on sobbing
forever.

Once a rose is stripped of its petals,
there is no adhesive that can put them back.

MARINERO MUERTO

Reymi Ferreira

Despeinados faroles y peces destruídos
a la orilla del mar, sirenas sollozando
sus penas junto a mi ventana y el musgo
ignorado invadiendo la noche de mis
entrañas.

Todo lo perdí yo que pude ser terrestre,
tener una guitarra y dar serenatas,
yo que pude ser pirata, comerciante
o simple perro.

Así es la vida y yo pasé flotando
sobre el mar mis desaventuras;
uno nace, crece y si no florece
a tiempo en primavera, el invierno
llenará después de sombra nuestra frente.

La hermosa chica que quería se
cambio de barrio y nunca supe mas
de ella, me hice a la mar y la
sal trago mi vida con sus peces.

Llegué a despojos sin culpas y sin gloria,
mi camiseta de marino es mi mortaja,
y lo unico que extraño en esta tumba
es el ardiente sol de aquel verano.

DEAD SAILOR

Reymi Ferreira

Overturned lanterns and dead fish
on the shore by the sea, sirens sobbing
their sorrows near my porthole and the moss
unnoticed invading the night
of my entrails.

I have lost all that could be terrestrial,
playing my guitar and singing my serenades,
I who could have been a pirate, a merchant
or just a dog.

That's the way life is, and I passed, floating
over the sea my misfortunes;
one is born, he grows and if he doesn't bloom
on time in the spring, the winter
will fill his face with shadows later.

The beautiful girl I loved
moved from the barrio and I never
heard any more of her, I set out on the sea
and the salt swallowed my life with its fishes.

I arrived at the spoils without glory or shame,
my sailor's shirt shall be my shroud,
and all I have left to mourn in this tomb
is the burning sun of that summer.

EL NEGRO DE LA ESQUINA

Reymi Ferreira

El negro de la esquina tiene su tambor,
el negro de la esquina tiene su lagarto,
ese negro, ese negro pecador.

Don Jeremias, le preguntó (una muchacha)
¿Qué hace usted para poder cantar así?

"Yo sólo soy encanto y poema;
—no me creas muchacha—yo sólo
canto con mi voz blanca y con mis
manos toco el mágico tambor azul.

Don Jeremias, le preguntaron (otras muchachas)
¿Por qué tiene usted los dientes amarillos como
el sol, porque su canto siempre alegra el corazón?

"Dios baila en mi pecho; a veces también
danzo yo; mi canto es un llamado sexual para
atraer a las arañas, es un canto de ansiedad
que busca llegar al oído tierno de las jovencitas.

Y así pasa la vida del negro Jeremias,
cantando con su gran boca y su tambor
y su lagarto, llenando de música la calle
y caminando,
siempre caminando y rodeado de muchachas;
ese negro, ese negro pecador.

THE BLACK MAN ON THE CORNER

Reymi Ferreira

The black man on the corner has his voodoo charm,
the black man on the corner has his drum,
that black man, that old black sinner.

Mr. Jeremiah (a little girl asks),
How do you sing like that?

I'm just a song and a magic spell;
you better believe it little girl,
I just sing with my white voice,
and with my hands I beat this magic blue drum.

Mr. Jeremiah (other little girls ask),
Why do your teeth shine yellow like the sun?
Why does your song make our hearts glad?

God is dancin' in my chest;
sometimes I even dance myself;
my song is a mating call for spiders,
and it's lookin' to find the tender ears of little girls.

And so goes the life of black Jeremiah,
singing with his big mouth and beating his drum,
Jeremiah with his voodoo charm, filling the streets with music
and strolling,
always strolling, surrounded by little girls,
that black man, that old black sinner.

FICTION

SECRET PAPERS FROM THE PACIFIC WAR

German Araúz

Nobody ever did figure out what kind of pull he had to land such an important position. Some said he was first cousin to the minister. Others claimed he was the director's brother-in-law. These and other speculations on the mysterious source of his influence were whispered up and down the corridors of the Ministry. The genealogists we called in for their expert knowledge of His Excellency the general's family tree said that he was related to him. The second mystery was his professional title. We randomly called him Señor Mareno, Don Pacific, Doctor Mareno, and even Your Honor—to see how he would react. Not the least gesture or twitch of an eyebrow confirmed or refuted any of our theories.

The in-processing clerk had his own version. He swore he had seen him a few years ago in a colonel's uniform, which was all the assistant payroll clerk needed to confirm his retired-officer theory. The warehouse dispatcher hooted at that hypothesis: "If he was in the army, it must have been the Salvation Army!" I had to laugh at the thought of him standing outside the Three Skulls every Friday, selling *Watch Towers,* but our resident Bible expert, the switchboard operator, took the opportunity to remind me that only the Jehovah's Witnesses sell *Watch Tower.*

Meanwhile, the aforementioned, that is, Pacific Mareno, maintained a stubborn silence, which we at first attributed to shyness. But in time our curiosity turned to suspicion and at last to fear. His refusal to engage in any kind of dialogue, even about office matters, led the auditor-in-chief to a logical conclusion: he had something to hide, and silence was his stratagem for hiding it. Whatever, any attempt—social or work-related—to get close to him met a stone wall of reserve. Our invitations were firmly and invariably rebuffed. The first invitation was to spend Friday night with the guys. We had a whole evening planned. What a menu—from the *Generality* at the Three Skulls to the initiation dance, cheek to cheek, with Brigitte at the Ochentita! The next was to celebrate his first paycheck—for good luck so it would last. Nothing moved him, not even an offer to let him in on an innocent chain letter with a big payoff for him. And then, when there was an argument between the Estrongo fans and the Bolivar fans, we asked him which team he rooted for. He answered, "I don't know anything about soccer."

Our tolerance reached its limit the day Jaqueline—*the* Jaqueline! the director's statuesque receptionist-secretary!—invited him, at our instigation, to a picnic at Achocalla. He replied that he didn't go in much for those nice little social gatherings.

All these rejections, as I have already stated, drove us from curiosity to fear and from fear to increasing dislike, aggravated by his disloyalty in the performance of his duties, because, as bad luck had it, Pacific Mareno had the all-important responsibility of allocating funds. He had every opportunity to look the other way when certain negligible "mistakes" occurred. I've watched more than one of his predecessors get filthy rich in that job. So what was the matter with him? He made the rest of us look bad.

Let's review the facts.

First aggression (two weeks after assuming his duties): two tax collectors, who had the careless habit of depositing all of their money into the strong box exactly as they had collected it, could not explain why the total amounts received considerably exceeded the sum of the amounts stated on the receipts. The result was a severe reprimand for the two tax collectors.

Second aggression (one week later): in addition to the above irregularities and others not worth mentioning here, Mareno (the supervisor) requested an audit from the director. The director, naturally, ignored the request. The result, from that time on, was that whenever the director entered the office, the supervisor ignored him.

Fourth aggression (after three months): in response to denunciations by "unidentified sources," the comptroller's office sent two auditors to do a meticulous inspection of the books. The result was that one of our accountants was removed from his duties, and two others were transferred to the archives.

Inevitably, the sum of these aggressions translated into a slow, pernicious diminution of our incomes. We were even driven to the humiliating extreme of having to sign IOU's at the Three Skulls. Something had to be done. If we didn't act now, we might all end up like the accountant. We therefore agreed that this was war. And to win, we needed to know, with absolute precision, who our enemy was and what his firepower was. We knew his name, but that was all. Therefore, the first thing to do was scrutinize his past: find out (1) if he was ever involved in politics and, if so, with what party (hopefully extremist); (2) if he was married and had a mistress at the same time (we discarded that hypothesis because of his bureaucratic habits); (3) if he liked soccer (he didn't) and what movies he went to (pornographic? shoot-'em-ups?). It was all a lamentable waste of time. Mareno was impenetrable. Nothing seemed to interest him. What kind of animal were we up against?

Then we persuaded, by means of a generous tip, one of the messenger boys to tail him. After five working days of indefatigable pursuit, we received one bit of interesting intelligence: he had lunch at the Magic Carrot, a vegetarian restaurant frequented by hippies, and everybody knows that vegetarianism is bound to be accompanied by other peculiar habits. We managed to identify his residence: a modest room on Catacora Street. None of this information, however, could be used effectively against him. We had to find something more substantial.

After twenty days, our young sleuth hit pay dirt: "I saw him having lunch with a boy."

"How old?"

"Between fifteen and twenty; it was hard to tell."

"Wha'd he look like?"

"Good looking, slender as a candle, man!"

(And having lunch, according to the messenger, wasn't all Moreno and the boy were doing together.)

"What? Are you shitting me, kid?"

"No! They did! You know his room on Catacora Street? They went there. And as they walked, I saw Mareno put his arm around him, and he was kissing him!"

"He's a pediatrist!" shrieked the switchboard operator.

"Pe-de-rast!" I corrected the dumb bitch.

So, this Pacific Mareno, the incorruptible *homo bureaucraticus*, as the director called him, was nothing but an ordinary homo.

"We can't allow such elements within our sacred precincts!"

"We have to do something about this!"

"Request an audit of his inanus!"

"*A-nus!*"

Finally, the chief—and that's why he *was* the chief—decided what we had to do: catch him *in flagrante.* But how?

It wasn't easy to convince the athletic file clerk to contribute to our cause, but at last, pocketing a healthy tip, he swore that what he would be doing was only for the defense of the dignity of mankind. As if we didn't know he spent his spare hours flirting with certain notorious transvestites.

At 10:00 A.M., D-day, Pacific Mareno, who, as in every act of his life, attended to his physical necessities with rigorous punctuality, took off his glasses; put his papers, ink, and pens in a desk drawer; closed and locked the drawer; and walked to the men's room. The file clerk, who was wearing a brand new silk shirt for the occasion, followed on Mareno's heels and disappeared behind the bathroom door. A moment later we heard noises and shouts and then a solid *thump.* Pacific Mareno emerged from the men's room, unruffled. He went back to his desk and resumed work. The file clerk did not reappear, and no one dared go into the men's room to investigate.

Ten minutes went by.

At last I went in myself. The file clerk was standing in front of the sink, splashing water on his face. His nose still showed signs of recent hemorrhaging. What he said was a model for concession: "I think we made a mistake."

It was a big mistake. The financial coordinator found out a few weeks later that the boy was Mareno's son. A native of Sucre, Pacific Mareno had had an administrative career and had been married and divorced there.

After that battle, or I should say debacle, our position became more serious. His reports flew over us with the deadly regularity of cannon fire. Our response was reduced to a series of ineffective forays, such as altering the figures on his receipts, spilling ink on the pages of his detailed analyses, making obscene telephone calls, smearing paste on his chair, and locking the men's room from the outside when he was in it. All we gained was that he learned not to leave documents on his desk, not to sit down until he inspected his chair, and not to receive telephone calls until the switchboard operator identified the caller. He even managed to modify his digestion so that he almost never had to go to the office bathroom. He didn't say a word, but his reports became progressively more destructive.

Something new had to be planned, a stroke capable of annihilating him. Otherwise, the war was lost. It was resolved unanimously that in order to avoid leaks, the next blow would be planned and executed by a special task force.

That afternoon, looking forward to a few leisurely and uninterrupted hours of perusing *Goals* magazine, I returned to the office earlier than usual. I was surprised to find that some of my colleagues, seized by a mysterious fit of punctuality, had arrived before me. They were gathered around Pacific Mareno's desk, and a locksmith was with them. I realized at once that this had to do with the task force. A bomb, I said to myself, and I went over to ask what they were doing. None of them, as we had previously agreed, satisfied my curiosity. All they said was no, this wasn't a bomb, and I should go back to my desk. The locksmith left the office, and they all did what I was doing: relaxed in their armchairs, worked, and waited.

Mareno came in at 2:23 P.M., punched the clock, and walked to his desk with cool indifference. He examined his chair, sat down, and pulled out his key chain. He pulled open the middle drawer, and for the first time I saw spasms on that stone sphinx face of his. No doubt there was something he saw in the middle drawer. And that something made such an impact that he jumped back, knocking over his chair. He rushed to the bathroom and threw up. We saw him throw up, because he hadn't locked the door behind him. Then he left the office. This, we had won. None of us, however, dared celebrate the victory.

A week passed with no signs of life from Pacific Mareno. Nobody had any information about him at personnel. Our initial doubts were evolving day by day into joyful hope. We made discrete inquiries at the vegetarian restaurant: he hadn't been back. We learned from a neighbor that he had left his rooms at Catacora Street in a hurry. He's gone back to Sucre was what everyone was saying, which amounted, declared the chief, to open desertion of his duties.

Ten days later we reached the final conclusion: victory! We had won the war, and we prepared for a joyous celebration at the Club de La Paz. Nothing less would do. The chief, who was a member there, offered to reserve a table big enough for the whole staff. We set the date for Friday night, so that later we could move the party to the Ochentita, cheek to cheek with Brigitte!

Friday morning we went into the office, and Pacific Mareno was there, bent over his papers, as if he had never moved from his desk. We knew then that this war; this horrible war, which we had thought was over and won, was only just beginning.

MANUELITO

Nicomedes Suárez Araúz

Manuelito was born in Loen, and every night since his birth a blue rider on a black horse would come up next to his bed and with his black machete would cut Manuelito's throat. Each night it inevitably happened.

In the morning, his mother, Dona Elcira, would find blood clots shaped like hearts, beating on her son's pillow. Worried, she would stay up all night watching over his sleep, hoping to find out the reason. Nevertheless, she never discovered any clues.

Each night the rider would arrive with his machete and each morning Dona Elcira would cast away little hearts of blood. Yet despite this odd nightly event, when Manuelito turned sixteen he looked like a full grown man. The night of his sixteenth birthday, anticipating the arrival of his nightly visitor, he stayed on watch, waiting for him with a machete. When the blue rider arrived, he approached Manuelito's bed and arched his body. He was about to give him the blow when Manuelito hit him first with his weapon, severing the rider's neck. A laughter of ringing glass bells invaded the room and echoed in his body.

Through the night the dried-up blood clots came back to life and began beating fast like the hearts of little birds.

Since then, Manuelito beheads the blue rider each night, and with every year that Manuelito adds to his age, the blue rider's age diminishes by one year. And the blood clots scattered amongst the grass, trees, ponds, gravel, and sand beaches beat weaker and weaker with every year that passes.

THE VOYAGER

Nicomedes Suárez Araúz

When the shadow of the wing of the house is two meters away from the wall of the house it is three in the morning. The stars then begin to peck every pore of the hands. That is why Don Luciano wakes up at that precise instant to ring the hour by beating on an old piece of rail hanging from the house's outer beam. Instead of using the metallic tubing intended for that purpose, Don Luciano uses the spine of his machete. He beats on the rail with such longing, as though his sleep were driving the blow, dong, dong, dong. Throughout the patio spreads a darkness of crows and a milky tulle. The songs of *sereres* (those birds of burnt mud) and the splashing of a cayman's tail ring in the ears.

On the floors of the rooms, stars are burning as though in a pan of dark oil, and now insomnia begins to penetrate the mind until it curdles into a lit candle.

Don Luciano lies awake, but he doesn't move. He feels that his eyes are growing to the limits of his skin and that they continue to extend until, finally, they explode like a tail lashing the river's waters.

Unable to find his machete, Don Luciano realizes they are ringing the fourth, the fifth, the sixth hour while the butterflies of dawn are flying under his skin.

In Loen it was said he died from taking an overdose of creosote and olive oil, and they noticed his eye sockets were empty. But yesterday when they buried him, they saw once again his eyes on his face, and they were so brilliant they burned like morning stars.

Tonight the shadow of the wing of the house is growing, covering small ants and army ants, covering the neighboring houses, covering the town, and finally reaching the cemetery. That shadow reaches Don Luciano, and he knows the hours that drift between the stars and understands how the light makes the clocks ring.

LAST MOMENTS

Gustavo Cardenas Ayad

He settled into the easy chair of oblivion to wait for the sun to set. Everything was over. The carnival of awards had suddenly stopped. The discolored diplomas and distinctions had nothing more to say. The toasts had all been drunk. All that the kisses and hugs had done for him was bruise his seventy-odd-year-old wrinkled skin. His unread books were being withdrawn from the store windows of his memory. Only he remained, with that dead smell, which continued to saturate him, that smell of formaldehyde which he had acquired on the afternoon when everybody remembered him.

It had all happened after his nap. He had wakened, panting and worried, from a dream. Looking out into the yard, he had seen his wife coming and said to her, "My dear, I dreamed I was dying."

"You're getting old if you're thinking that," she answered.

He kept looking out into the yard, breathing rapidly. It had never crossed his mind before, and now it had come to him in an afternoon nap. Everybody else in the city had evidently had the same nap and the same dream, and the proof came straight to his front door: a bundle of congratulations on his first book, the book he had written when he was barely twenty, when he was still unaware of the trouble words can cause. Looking through the telegrams and honorary degrees, he wondered what inexcusable delay in the mail . . . how many times around the world . . . no, they were all dated that day and the signatures were still wet. He smiled and sighed, "Better late than never . . ."

"But why," he continued smiling, "so suddenly and all at the same time?" In the afternoon drowsiness he shared his awards and honors with his wife the way a child shares a sack of new toys.

As he grew tired of reading and rereading them, he caught a strange, strong odor in the air. He got his wife to help him take a bath, but the smell got worse. He sprinkled himself with cologne and put on fresh clothes, but the smell stayed.

There was loud knocking at the front door. More packets arrived: more honorary degrees, more titles and distinctions and letters of recognition, coming from every corner of the country. "Shut the front door," he called, because, he reasoned, this was not normal. But the constant knocking finally changed his mind, and he asked them to just leave it open, and so his house turned into a parade of every class of person from all over the world, arriving at all hours of the day and night, standing in line to wish him well and give him titles, letters, and honors.

On the third day, tired of offering his cheek to be kissed, his hand to be shaken, he got up and started out into the street, supported by his old cane. The street was decorated all over with strips of paper, and people were congregated within a radius of twenty blocks. "This must be a religious festival or national holiday," he thought, but it didn't take him long to realize that it was all in his honor.

"For an author of ninety-two books," whispered the mayor, pinning the medal on the city's favorite and most brilliant son, "this was the very least we could do."

"History and literature are honored here today," declared the president, perforating the faded breast of his old linen suit.

"You are my favorite author," said all the beauty queens, printing his wrinkled forehead with carmine and giving him roses and jasmines.

Without changing countenance, he wept; he thanked them all without exuberance, because throughout his ancient body the smell of death kept growing.

Perfuming himself with sandalwood water and cistern water, he decided that all this bother was a conspiracy of all the storybook figures he had raised from the dust of oblivion, now crowding into the streets and parks of the city, and he came to the conclusion that what the dead really deserve is eternal silence.

He kept silent as more titles and distinctions continued to arrive and new editions of his books overflowed the bookshelves and window displays.

That afternoon, when it was all over and everybody had acknowledged his accomplishments, for the first time he resigned himself to living with the cadaverous smell. "It's too late for everything," he told his wife as he sat down for the last time in his hundred-year-old chair.

"You must be really getting old," she answered, "if thinking about that is all you're living for."

With the weight of the honorary degrees in his lap and the medals on his chest, he got ready for the last scene, convinced that only the sky and the sea have the power to lose themselves in the infinite. He looked at the horizon, now very near. The sun began to slip slowly from the curtain of sky.

ALL THE BONES OF DEATH

Gustavo Cardenas Ayad

When the city was founded in 1612 and the first stone was laid in the Plaza de Armas, at the same time the first stone of the cemetery was also placed, in full consciousness of the fact that dying was as necessary as being born.

The city grew by leaps and bounds with towering edifices and winding streets. The houses encircling the plaza slowly became venerable two-story buildings with galleries below and balconies above. Only the cemetery, spanning the length of five centuries, was growing out in a horizontal fashion. Multilevel sepulchers were not permitted, as it was considered poor taste to bury one dead person on top of another.

Over the vast, holy ground, a man trudged all afternoon, reading the epitaphs and names, half-erased by eroding inclemencies over time. More than once he leaned down to decipher some all-but-illegible inscription that was scrawled over one of the crosses that were lying broken on the mounds of earth. As one who looks for an address, a street name, a house number, he studied and perused the writings on the tombs.

The first day, he searched from north to south. The next day he went from east to west. The third day, more agitated than ever, he decided that the only way to find the tomb would be to make the rounds in a spiral direction, from the outskirts to the inside. That day dawned, and his anxiety and desire led him through twisting, mournful paths. When dusk came he at last read the long-sought name, the last name, and the date inscribed on a solid, discolored cross. He adjusted his glasses and read the inscription over and over.

His eyes grew moist, behind the lenses of his glasses. They looked like two cankers, staring straight ahead at one point in the distance. "I have returned," he said in a soft voice, though there was no one there to whom it would matter. From a bag he took a flower, almost crushed; he fluffed up the petals as best he could and leaned it at the base of the cross.

"Now that I know where you rest, you'll have me here every day," he promised as he broke into sobs.

He left with a tiredness brought on by his fifty years, remembering, without trying to block anything out, reminiscing about the days spent with her, the endless nights lying with her alone on the couch—then the shock of learning that she was going to marry someone else.

He recalled the blush of color on her cheek, the sweet smell of her breath on that terrible afternoon when she'd told him she could not marry him, that she could not go against her father. "I will return," he'd said then, convinced he would have to go away. "I can't imagine you in the arms of another," he'd argued.

Now everyone was dead; that was the only truth. He assumed it to be. The other man had fallen from his horse on returning home, when the street lights had suddenly come on. Her father had succumbed to a heart attack. Her hour had come one night while undressing for her bath, and she was found two days later, surrounded by a huge cloud of vapor.

But he had returned. He discarded the idea of digging up her body, according to an ancient tradition. "I will shower your tomb with geraniums from your own balcony," he promised.

And so it was that the next day, his arms full of fresh-cut geraniums, he conducted himself to the cemetery under the perplexed and watchful eyes of the surrounding neighborhood.

First he cut away the weeds that were growing around the head of the grave; then, when he was able to plant the memorial flowers, he noticed, surprised, that water was seeping out of the surface hole which he had dug. In vain were his attempts to staunch the flow; the water came out in spurts and began to saturate the holy ground.

Desperately he left at a run, shouting for help. The people saw him passing by like a flash of lightning through the streets of the little town. Poor man, bad luck for him.

"I think he's gone crazy," said one woman.

"What're you saying?" asked the mayor.

"It looks like the sea is breathing through the cemetery," he answered.

"How do you expect us to believe that, when you have just recently arrived here?" the mayor asked.

"I don't know what else to say," answered the man.

At that moment, some neighbors arrived who confirmed his story—in the cemetery it was raining from underneath, and the unearthing of bones and whole skeletons had already begun. Coffins and funeral clothing were trying futilely to attach themselves to the roots of trees which were now toppling over as they found themselves noisily uprooted from solid ground.

"It's the end of the world."

"If you'll look, sir, the crosses are floating like boats on the plains of the graveyard."

"I think it's the end of the town. What are we going to do with all of our dead?" sobbed a woman.

The people went on mourning over their dead while the strange cataclysm continued.

At the end of six days, the man returned, with the notion that it was over. There were no traces left of the municipal cemetery. All that could be seen was a vast plain strewn with a huge and variant quantity of gleaming bones.

Many people wanted to reconstruct the bodies of their dead, and they spent years comparing the sizes of bones, looking for a gold tooth, a mutilated arm or leg, a medallion, a religious relic, or a certain caliber of bullet. He, guided by the fragrance, tried at first to find some bones with a scent of geraniums. Gropingly he searched from north to south, from east to west, in a spiral, from heaven to earth. "My love is stronger than death," he consoled himself.

Unfortunately, neither he nor anyone else was able to put together enough bones to be able to say, "This is my beloved."

Forming an endless labyrinth of exodus, the people could be seen marching in interminable caravans out of the town. As he stared unblinkingly at the immense plain of desert colors, he was convinced that he was completely alone. Now he was looking at all of it as if into a glass, where he could see all of the bones of Death. Over his head, he could see the vultures, flying in slow circles.

HALF-WIT

Homero Carvalho

The sun trap, placidly occupying every place that was unpro-
tected by shade, spread out like a huge pond that extended so far that
it seemed free and separate at the base of the ground, which seemed
to have escaped it at noontime. One needed to go only a few steps
to discover it was not so; it had made its way even down to the
coolest corners and was creeping up to the highest walls. A sun trap
is like that. That hot, heavy air, laden with troubles and problems,
immobilized the little town after the lunch hour, keeping it in a life-
less time-space, among regulated snores and stolen kisses, lost in
dreams. Men and animals slept the sleep of the righteous at this hour
when the forest breathed its heavy breath over objects and houses.

Slowly, without hesitation or haste, man regained his life—the
bath, the cafe, the job—the inhabitants went back to their routines.
In the spacious main street some little boys played with their toy
guns, reenacting scenes from the latest Mexican movie that had
been showing for the past two weeks in the only movie theater in
San Gabriel.

Farther away along the brick walkway, he stood, leaning against
a pillar of the mayor's mansion, in a shady spot, fighting the heat.
He was turning over and over in his hand a thin, white cylinder; like
a little tree, he thought, that will never flower or shed leaves, a tree,
a pillar, some other pillar, they're all alike. At the square base where
he sat, his little cylinders were leaning like little sleeping men at
siesta hour. A half-moon of smoke, like a bee's trail, circled around
him, flirting with the sunshine, chatting with the protective shadows
from the awning.

"I'm learning to smoke today."

One of the hand-rolled cigarettes fell over and landed on the dirty
folds of his shirt, hoping to be lifted to his deformed lips, the lips of
the half-wit. The shirt, which in former, better times had been white,
was now stained with blotches of yellow. His skin flinched at the
tiny points of heat, the hundreds of little needle pricks, as he brought
the cigarette up to his mouth. The first puff choked him, but he
consoled himself. There would be others. And he would learn. He

looked at the man who had given him this marvelous thing, that nice grown-up, and he tried to thank him with his split tongue and incomprehensible lisp.

Later he wondered why the man did that, but it was too late to ask. As he brought a cigarette to his lips again, he coughed and told himself in answer that what he held in his hand was the same thing that grown-up men had, and that was enough for him. Other times it had been candy and gum, but this was even better. The cigarette butt flew through the air and landed sadly in the gutter; now no longer the chosen one, it would lie with its buddies, butts from other smokers, and from himself, especially, remains of the cigarettes that the man had given him. He liked to look at the happy ashes that scattered through space when he breathed deeply, the better to see the red glow that slowly advanced until it burned his fingers. Wreathed in smiles, he lost himself among the trees, stopping from time to time to pick up whatever he thought was interesting.

At nightfall he went back down the hill to occupy his spot in the main window of the cafe. He liked listening to the conversations of the big guys; he called them that because he'd heard other people of the town call them that, scornfully. He didn't think of them that way because sometimes they gave him coins for his pains. That night he noticed that they were nervous, and the local shop owner had not thrown him out yet with his "You half-wit shithead, get on up the hill," which was the usual expletive from the owner. He picked up a cigarette butt—oh, this was really a nice one—and he began to taste the difference in flavor from the ones he'd had; he'd just now noticed the brand of it.

"Who was the son of a bitch?"

"Nobody knows, Don Miguel. I don't think he's from here; nothing like this has ever happened in San Gabriel before. Pigeon-Toes' little girl, the poor little thing, she's in the hospital bleeding her little life out."

"That dirty son of a whore . . . and those sons of bitches, what've they done about it? Gone lookin' for him? Caught anybody?"

"No, Don Miguel, nobody knows nothing. She'd go out to play everyday by herself up on the mountain—shit!"

The howl of a black alley cat that he surprised from its lair and which disappeared behind the corner blotted out their words. He could hear no more, and he moved away, ambling toward the movie theater, hoping someone would let him in. Unsuccessful, he walked on toward the school, stuffing his pockets with cigarette butts, until at last he snuggled himself into a favorite corner. He listened for a while to the scampering of the rats on the roof and told himself that he would never get used to the nasty whining of mosquitoes around his face.

His face to the sky, eyes closed, he felt millions of little red points pricking his pupils. "Stars that everybody has for his own," he said to himself. Suddenly he opened his eyes, but he had to close them again; the big yellow disc above was hurting them from its height of transparent blue. Turning over in the grass and rubbing his eyes, he discovered a tree he'd never seen before; it seemed wondrous and rare. He came here every day; this was his place, his big house; here he could reproduce in his mind movie scenes. He knew every centimeter of the neighborhood, and this new member he'd never seen until today, a new friend. He caressed it. "You'll be the son of Tarzan, you giant tree," he said, stroking a huge leaf that would shelter him against the rain.

The thought of this new friend filled him with happiness, and for the first time, he smoked a whole cigarette. That man the other night had given him a whole pack; he couldn't get to sleep thinking about being here in his big house, as he called it, this place just outside of town, and lighting the first cigarette in the company of his plant friends; he hadn't invited the others.

A sudden muffled cry prevented him from continuing his reveries. He hid himself among his friends, silencing the rustle of his body as he crept to the clearing. There he saw strong hands jerking at the little blue panties of a small girl who was crying. The man was speaking softly to her, promising her candies, dolls, saying that he wasn't going to hurt her. Now he caressed her little bottom, undressing her until she lay sobbing and naked on the ground, covering her face with her hands.

What the half-wit saw next reminded him of his mother, when they'd lived in the little room by the cemetery and she'd lain with different men, ignoring his presence; and when he'd get up from his cot, she'd tell him to go to bed and not watch. But he had watched anyway, and he'd listened. But this was different. His mother had liked it; he was sure she'd liked it, for she would hug and kiss the man with the thousand faces and make little moans, barely audible utterings, asking for more, more. But this one was screaming and crying. "No, no, it hurts! Please stop, stop . . ." Besides, he thought, she didn't have big beautiful breasts like his mother's, whose had pleased him so much to caress.

He stayed rooted to the spot until dark came on.

"If you tell Mommy or Daddy anything we did, *I'll kill you*—and I won't give you any more candies or let you sneak into the movies anymore."

"No, no, I won't tell anybody, but it hurts . . ."

"Hush, be quiet, and now you know, if you say a single word to anyone, I'll kill you."

The man went away. The girl looked down at her hands and wiped the blood off her legs and then went away crying.

Sitting at his special window at the cafe, he decided that the man had tricked the girl and that he wasn't going to give her either the doll or the candies.

"Don Miguel, another one, another little girl, violated, up on the mountain!"

"Well, this is the last straw; we have to find that pervert. Why, if this goes on, it'll not be safe for any of our daughters to go out of their houses without something happening to 'em. And those shit-eatin' sons of bitches not doin' a damn thing!"

They cursed all through the night, judging and sentencing the culprit to the most hideous punishments. Public burning in the middle of the square with green logs—no, that was too good for him; he needed to be cut up in little pieces or impaled on a stake. The sound of sick, sonorous laughter cut short their deridings, which then gave way to insults and taunts.

"Get out of here, half-wit moron."

"Lispy."

"Broken-tongue."

He kept on laughing, and his laughter continued until he had lost himself at the schoolhouse, where he laughed until his chest hurt. He knew why he was laughing, and he knew everything. He was smarter than the smartest of all of them, and he would not tell. Let them rot, let them cudgel their brains out asking themselves who it was. That night he smoked two cigarettes and slept.

"What's going on with that half-wit?" The people wondered as he laughed and laughed.

He would stop by to listen to the gossiping of the townspeople as they continued to talk about the rapes, and he would interrupt them with cackles of laughter and idiotic mocking gestures, eluding their blows and their kicks and their insults. Those were the happiest days of his life: He was important, he told himself, repeating it over and over. He couldn't sleep from thinking about the parents of those little girls, thinking that they too probably couldn't sleep, as they lay awake inventing all sorts of ways to punish the culprit, asking themselves a thousand times and a thousand times again who it could be, while he smoked and laughed. Those days, he would wander through the town, not going to his place; he feared that his plant friends would throw it at him—that he was the witness and that he should tell what he'd seen and heard. No, he didn't want to; he wanted to keep on being important, being the only one who knew who the man, the violator, was. For not one of the big guys, not Pigeon-Toes, not the shopkeeper, not the carpenter, not even the priest who knows everything knew what he wasn't telling.

Feeling bored, sitting on a bench at the plaza, he stared at some students who were kicking around a homemade soccer ball. He was annoyed; he'd found only a few cigarette butts, smoked down to the filter, and couldn't get anything out of them. Now he could hear the students saying they were going down to the schoolhouse to smoke, and it was just the time when he usually spread out his mat for a nap. His gaze roved everywhere, looking for cigarette stubs . . . but nothing. His eyes brightened at the sight of Dantico; he was the man who'd given him his first cigarette, who passed him one every day. He remembered the day Dantico had handed him a whole pack; he remembered what he'd seen the next evening on the mountaintop, from his big house, and Dantico didn't know that he'd seen him threatening, promising, raping the little girl. But he, the half-wit, hadn't told on him because that man was his friend, the one who always gave him candies and cigarettes and sometimes let him sneak into the movies. His friend, the ticket taker, the rapist—and now he was hoping that he'd give him a cigarette, as usual. At length, he passed by him, followed him around, then asked him.

"Don't bother me, you moron, you shit-headed half-wit. I'm in a hurry. Anyway, I'm not your father," Dantico answered.

He didn't have a father, he'd never had one, at least he'd never known about it, but what did that matter? All he wanted was a cigarette. Why did the man not give him one? Why did he shove him? He'd never done that before. The half-wit ran, he cursed, he kicked at a water can. White-faced, he arrived at the cafe; his lisping tongue seemed to be stumbling all over itself as he stammered out his speech: "I saw him, Don Miguel, there in my big house on the mountain, with the carpenter's daughter—"

"Talk slower, half-wit. With your messed-up tongue I can't understand a thing you're sayin'. Hey, come here. This half-wit, I don't know what he's sayin'."

And the people gathered around and listened . . .

"I saw him; it was Dantico. He pulled her little blue panties off, he promised her candies and dolls, and she screamed and cried. I swear it was him, and nobody knew but me, believe me . . ."

"This half-wit is talkin' foolishness. He's a liar! Why, Don Miguel, Dantico's a good boy, the half-wit's probably mad at him for not lettin' him into the movies . . . Say, you know what? This moron must be the culprit, and we've all been thinkin' him a saint. Why, he's nothing but a pervert—don't you see? That's why he's been laughing at us all this time, laughing at our daughters, makin' fun of them, the nasty lecher!"

He cried, he begged, he got down on his knees and swore his innocence before Pigeon-Toes, who, egged on by some gossipy old women, went to get his bullwhip. Pigeon-Toes vented all his fury, his betrayal, his father-love enraged into vengeance, and he counted each day that he'd waited for that moment with each stroke of the scourge. After a couple hundred blows, the carpenter replaced him, with hands accustomed to wielding hammer and wood, and before long, the skin was flaying off the back of the unfortunate boy.

"So, you half-wit moron, you son of a whore, you do this? To me, who's fed you?" And the whip whistled through the air with its promise that it would bury itself in the tortured skin of the half-wit. Students came then with vegetables and fruits, even bones, to hurl at him; and the old women cursed the day he'd been born, recalling his mother, saying they'd been glad when they found out she'd been murdered by one of her lovers.

"And you, Mr. Shopkeeper, don't interfere. The town is getting its justice."

"But, Don Miguel, this is a crime. This much and more he deserves to get."

The relatives trickled away; the school friends wandered off; finished were the insults, the hurled vegetables and fruits and bones. The vengeance had cooled and the street was empty. Alone with his wounds, with his split tongue and his deformed lips, the half-wit begged for angels to come, angels like the ones in the pictures the priest had shown to his catechism class. He waited in agony and pain for the arrival of the lady with the scythe, the one who must be the boss lady for all the teachers. He would go to heaven; he was good. Why had they done this?

A woman dressed in men's shoes and light-colored trousers stood before him.

"No more now," she said.

Her ironic smile soothed him. She watched him for a few seconds, stuck a cigarette between his bleeding, deformed lips . . . then disappeared.

COPPER PUMPKINS

Viviana Limpias Chavez

If they had only understood that fate is not just winning the
lottery or drowning in a flood on Good Friday, they might have real-
ized that fate was traveling with them on that city bus and was actu-
ally sitting next to me. But what did they care about her and her
deep black eyes or her pair of embossed copper pumpkins, reflecting
the destiny of everyone who, by chance, at eleven o'clock in the
morning, had caught the only city bus crossing the seventh district
with a Gypsy on it.

Maybe nobody guessed that, woven into her purple dress, a bright
chain of knowledge sparkled and danced to an unknown music.

For most of them, the purple dress, the fat white hands, and the
long tendrils of black hair that swung like pendulums in backward-
running clocks had no significance. If some few passengers felt any
suspicion, they concealed it. Their thoughts were as crammed
together as they themselves were on the bus. Preoccupied with the
next hour of their lives, they failed to live that minute and enjoy the
unearthly and radiant beauty of the Gypsy. But she intrigued me like
a character in a story.

I watched her sitting matriarchally on her bus seat as if it were a
throne. And no one recognized her as a passenger from another time.
Maybe it was the cataracts of day-to-day living that kept them from
seeing fate seated in front of them. I couldn't take my eyes off her
copper pumpkins. They seemed to come to life before me. First it
was the shimmer of purple all around them, then her rosy nipples
about to erupt. Her breasts became crystal balls, transparent as water,
and in them destiny whirled at dizzying speed before my eyes.

I looked upon the Haymarket fire of 1868; Lawrence of Arabia's
lost dagger in a petrified sand dune; three reels of Charlie Chaplin's
The Tramp, misplaced in 1916; a lance thrown by one of Boves'
cavalry in the battle of Pitayo, lodged from ear to ear in the skull of
a Spaniard; Pontiac's sandal after he was assassinated in 1769; Roa
Sierra's hand taking the pistol they offered to him to kill Gaitan with
on the ninth of April, 1948; the blind eyes of Borges, lost in a
labyrinth, searching through the *Divine Comedy* for a key to get out;

the atrophied jaws of a gold bug, chewing each night on a Chibcha king's mummy; and, last of all, I saw the blood spurting from a small hole opened by a rifle bullet in my back.

In the millionth of a second that it takes an eyelid to twitch, the Gypsy had disappeared. I got off the bus and starting running. Three blocks later I saw soldiers stopping the bus and making passengers get off one by one. To my surprise, the Gypsy was getting off; then after her, I got off. I ran desperately toward the same corner where I crouched, hiding and watching. There was a shot, and I fell dead. Two copper pumpkins rolled across the dirty sidewalk.

INSIDE THE MINE

Alfonso Gumucio Dagron

The boy ran down the alley between two rows of adobe huts, zigzagging to avoid the smelly puddles, leaping to the left and to the right the way he always did, his damp little feet slipping in his loose sandals. On the last stretch he would have to duck just at the right moment to avoid the tin gutter that hung down from one of the eaves and had gashed open more than one forehead. The words throbbed in his head: "Nogales says you have to hide because they're coming in from behind the Union building."

Or better, "Papa, Nogales says you've got to make yourself scarce, you've got to evaporate." He saw the gutter straight ahead, ducked, and knew, as it brushed across his hair, that once again he had outwitted the treacherous metal. He straightened up, and his hand hung onto the corner of the wall so as to take the curve without losing speed; down the slope the truck-tire soles of his rubber sandals braked. Then, crash, he slammed into the back of one of them. They were already in the house. They had come into town from everywhere, not just from behind the Union building. The soldier stumbled, and the barrel of his M-1 jammed into the loose mud between the adobe bricks.

"Stupid shit!" growled the sergeant from a few yards away. "That's not a candle you're holding, soldier, that's a rifle! What? Scared by a little kid?"

The soldier turned pale and snarled at the kid; then, sitting down with the rifle between his legs, he pulled a wire from a pocket in his uniform, carefully unwound it, and began cleaning the dirt out of the barrel. The boy recognized the weeping inside the house and tried to get in, but the sergeant blocked his way. He could see his mother sobbing where she sat on the edge of her cot. There was an officer with a mustache. It was that officer, he was sure, who was making her cry. He raised his head. The sergeant was looking at him. No escape now.

"You live here?"

"Yes, sir," he answered, reserved.

"You can't go in. The lieutenant is interrogating your mamma."

"Yes, sir."

He sat down beside the door and waited. Interrogating? Gating? Baiting? He peeped in between the sergeant's boots. He saw his mother go over to the stove, heard her blow on the fire to get it going, heard her stir the boiling soup in the pot, and saw her use her apron to dry the steam off her hands and face . . . and the tears. Or maybe he was just imagining. The lieutenant's boot appeared a few inches from his face, on the step. The lieutenant gave an order to the sergeant, and the sergeant trotted off with the soldier. The lieutenant looked at the sun, looked down the alley, looked at the ground, looked at him.

"Where's your papa?" he said, tugging at his mustache.

"Donno, sir," he stammered.

"What?"

"Isn't he here, in the house, sir?"

"No. Right now we're looking for him . . . so he can settle a problem that's come up with the Union radio station."

The radio station, that's where the boy had come from. There, Nogales had told him clearly, "Run home and tell your father they've come in again." Again, once more, again, the uniforms had come.

His mother came to the door, wiping her hands and frowning. "Where have you been, you little rascal? Leaving me here by myself all morning! Come in here and eat your broth!" She dragged him inside by the ear, without hurting him.

The lieutenant stayed outside, striding back and forth in front of the open door. The sun went in and out each time the lieutenant passed. Some shots were heard in the distance, and the lieutenant paused. Silence. Again the lieutenant paced. Near the stove, another soldier was squatting on the floor, sipping some broth out of a cup, keeping an uneasy eye on the sun as it went in and out beyond the doorway and the huge shadow of the lieutenant. The soldier cut off a bit of potato with his spoon and sipped the last of his broth.

"Thank you, Señora." He shyly returned the cup.

"I'll give you some more. You must be hungry after marching so far."

"Oh, we were real close—" he stopped himself, as if he had already said too much.

"Have some more anyway. You're poor, too, like us. You must be hungry." And she filled his cup again.

"Thank you, Señora," he repeated, embarrassed, looking out the corner of his eye at the doorway, the shadow going by, the sun going in and out.

His mother served him a cup, too, filled to the brim, crammed with potatoes. "Where on earth have you been?" she asked him, lowering her voice.

"At the radio station, Mamma, with Nogales—"

"Shh!" She pointed toward the door. Shadow, sun, shadow . . . sun. "And wasn't your papa with Nogales?" she asked anxiously.

No, he shook his head. The soldier didn't seem to hear a thing; his face was enveloped in steam from the broth.

"Ay! Surely they haven't caught him alone somewhere!" She was worried, unhappy.

Shadow, sun, shadow . . . shadow.

"Corporal!" It was the voice of the lieutenant.

"Yessir, Lieutenant!" the soldier leaped to his feet, not knowing what to do with the cup in his hands.

"Go see where that jerkoff sergeant of yours has gone. He should have been back thirty minutes ago," he declared, exaggerating the authority in his voice.

"Yessir, Lieutenant!" he said, and off he ran, passing the lieutenant in the doorway.

"Boy!" This time he was talking to him. "What's your name?" he asked in a friendly tone.

"His name is Jaimito," his mother intervened. "What kind of job do you want from him, Lieutenant?"

"Jaimito, I want you to go get your papa. I'm sure you know where he is."

"Yes, sir."

"Ahah! You do know where he's hiding."

"No, sir."

"Then why did you say, 'Yes, sir'? Tell him, when you find him, that I'll be staying right here until he comes. I'll be talking with your mamma. Tell him that."

"Yes, sir."

"And tell him not to be stupid, not to pull any dumb stunts like he did in '67 . . . Go on, what are you waiting for?"

"Yes, sir." He looked at his mother. He saw worry in her face. In the faintest movement of her lips, he thought he read a plea.

A gray cold was settling on the mining district. There was silence in Alonso Square. The four entrances were guarded by soldiers. Now the silence was breaking up, first a noise, a murmur, then from time to time a shout. The soldiers didn't try to stop the first women from entering the square. The women crossed it diagonally, going toward the Union building, sweating, carrying their babies with them. When the last of them had come in, filling the square, the shouts grew louder.

"What have we done, anyway?"

"They aren't satisfied to take our radio from us—they're taking prisoners again. What for? What's the reason?"

"They've even cut off our water and electricity! What right do they have to do that?"

"And they've closed the commissary! No meat, no rice, no sugar. What are we supposed to eat? Are they trying to starve us?"

"And throwing our husbands in jail?"

"They've arrested our leaders in the city, and here they're persecuting us, too, taking prisoners!"

The window on the second floor of the Union building opened. An army officer appeared, flanked by a few civilians. "Ladies! This mining district, as well as five others," he was taking his time, "has been declared a military zone by the supreme government. Mi-li-tar-y zone," he repeated.

"This is a mining zone, not a military zone!" a woman shouted.

"Which means," the officer continued calmly, "that the demonstration which you people have organized is illegal; it is being directed by foreign agents, and it constitutes an act of insubordination against the military authorities . . ."

"Booo!"

"Give us back our Union building! Give us back our radio!"

"Set our leaders free! Let our workers out of jail!"

"Ladies!" A microphone had now been turned on, amplifying the officer's voice. "Don't make it necessary for me to clear the square by force. You must go back to your respective homes until a new order arrives."

"And what are we going to eat when we get there? What are we going to give our children?"

"What are we going to use for water to cook with?"

"Ladies! We are in a state of siege, and this demonstration is a provocation. The government knows that extremists are operating here, stirring up the workers—"

"No extremists! Miners, workers!"

"Extremists," the officer continued, beginning to lose his temper, "who have come in from the outside for the Miners' Union Convention and have persuaded the workers to reelect the same leaders—"

"Where are the extremists? Show us one extremist among your prisoners! Show us one of your prisoners who isn't a worker!"

"Ladies! I will not tolerate any more provocation! When your husbands return to their jobs and the situation is normalized, I guarantee you that the martial law will be lifted. But if the general strike continues, I am responsible for keeping order in this district."

"The workers struck because the government arrested the leaders elected by the rank and file."

"We declared a general strike after you occupied the mines, after you seized our Union building, after you took over our radio."

The officer wasn't listening anymore. He disappeared behind the window, followed by his escort of civilians. Moments later a soldier closed the window. The women were withdrawing in groups, talking excitedly. The crowd was thinning out and disappearing in the streets of the mining village. Gray cold had settled on the whole area.

This time no lights appeared one after the other from the mine. No outlines of the heads and caps of the miners could be seen emerging as the wagon slid toward the exit of the mine. This time, no, there was no wagon. There was no orderly procession, and the lamps of the mining caps could be seen bunched together, to the right and to the left, far into the darkest part of the tunnel.

The soldiers watching the mouth of the mine avoided getting too close, and the boy made it inside without any trouble. Here the dark was total. Your eyes didn't get used to it. You brought your lamp, or you didn't see. That's what he was thinking as he groped deeper into the tunnel, holding onto the guide rail. Up ahead there was a light. He kept walking until he bumped into a miner with a cap and a lamp.

"Have you seen my papa, comrade?" He used the word his father used with the workers.

The man straightened up, took his hand, and led him deeper into the mine. "We'll look for him together." The man's boots echoed loudly, striking the puddles.

The boy had seldom entered the mine, and only with his father. Now it was different. They had cut off the light. There was no noise of shovels or drills. The tunnels were not trembling, and no dynamited walls were crumbling. Now it was the silence he heard, a silence occasionally broken by distant murmurs that bounced from corridor to corridor, cleverly finding their way in the dark through a network of levels, corridors, tunnels, halls, and shafts. The miner's boots trod in the puddles of sulfate water. A dry, cracked hand suddenly pulled the boy into a little room walled with boards. Newspapers were strewn all over. Light . . . men.

"Your father was here," the miner told him calmly. A typewriter, papers, and an old wood table were visible. Somebody jerked a paper out of the typewriter.

"There!" A miner held the paper up. "Listen to this."

Report from the Strike Committee, District 4:

Comrade soldier, have you ever once asked yourself why you have to put up with cold and hunger standing guard at these mines? And what's worse, have you asked yourself why you have to aim your rifle and threaten . . . ?

"Your papa was here." The hand was dry and cracked, warm.

Maybe you don't know, comrade soldier, that we miners have many children, that we have mothers and wives, that they will be left orphans, without any means of support, if you obey your generals' orders to massacre us . . .

"Come on." Once again he let himself be led into the dark. The voice that was reading grew faint.

We seek better salaries, just as you do. We are hungry, too, and since, like you, we, too, suffer from the cold . . .

Splash, splash, splash went the boots in the puddles. His sandals splashed, too. They were soaked through with sulfate water, but he wasn't thinking of that. Far ahead, lights were moving about. Splash, splash, splash. Silence. Another wooden door. Light filtered from between the boards. The one hand, warm, didn't let go; the other hand knocked gently.

We housewives have organized in response to the criminal methods of this anti-worker, anti-national government, which has sold out to imperialism, closed down our commissaries, and left thousands of households without the necessities for living . . .

The miner led him into the room, where they met a few people, both men and women. "Good evening, comrade. How are you feeling?" He was speaking to a woman lying in a corner on a makeshift mattress; he recognized her.

"I'm all right, comrade, thank you" —it was Domitila, from the Housewives Committee—"considering the circumstances, but the other women have helped me in everything."

And now the army has blocked the entrances and exits to the mine. They mean to annihilate both the leaders and the rank and file workers who are inside the mine directing the struggle and protecting their own lives . . .

"Oh, my God, twins!" exclaimed the miner, laughing. Then he frowned. "But in this difficult situation . . ."

. . . an appeal to all the housewives in all the mining camps to organize meals and collect provisions for our comrades.

Domitila listened to the end of the appeal. Lying next to her, wrapped up like two loaves, were the newborns.

"My God, twins!" The miner couldn't believe it.

"Are you looking for your papa?" Domitila asked him.

He nodded, not taking his eyes from the babies.

"Oh, my boy!" she sighed; then she said to the miner with the warm hand, "Go ahead and take him to his papa. Take him."

He still had to walk a long, long way in the double night of the tunnel, with the dripping sulfate, in the double silence broken by the splash, splash, splash of the boots. His legs were tired, his body was going to sleep. He walked with his eyes shut, letting himself be led.

"Your father was here. Your father was here," the miner would say softly. And the boy thought about Domitila, so fat when he had seen her a few days earlier. How many children did Domitila have now? The hand let go of him in a lighted area of the tunnel, more spacious than before. Miners were walking around, talking, meeting. The warm hand brushed across his face and pointed. He saw his father on the ground next to another miner at the other end of the lighted area, almost in the shadow. He went up to him, crouched at his side, and looked at him for a long time. He thought he still needed to give him the message from Nogales. And the one from the lieutenant, too. And tell him that they took Nogales away with the radio in a Caiman truck. And about Domitila . . . He removed the miner's cap. The lamp was broken. He looked at his father's face, his clenched lips, his hair wet with dirt, his cheeks black and bruised. He touched his shoulder, gently, with his fingers. With his eyes, he examined his body. There was a shoe missing. He stayed crouched next to his father, watching him, keeping him company, resisting.

The boy walked unhurriedly along the alley between the adobe walls. At the end, he ducked his head indifferently and felt the corner of the tin gutter, still bent, brush against his hair. The lieutenant was there at the door.

"Well, now do you know where your papa is?" he asked, as he had asked before.

"Yes, sir." Inside the hut there was silence.

"Yes, sir." He thought he could hear the breathing of his mother. "My papa says if you want to speak with him . . . he says if you want to . . . you can come look for him inside the mine."

He sensed his mother closing her eyes tight.

THE LAW

Amilkar Jaldín

It's still light when we get to the outer limit. It doesn't matter what road one takes: all of them begin where the plain ends and all lead to the same place, the house in the middle of the circle.

"Who would invent such a law, eh?"

The guy with the cymbals seems not to have heard me, nor does the drummer, who, carrying his instrument as usual, keeps on walking. The other two, one with the music box and the other with the castanets and other percussions, just look at me.

So what, I think. Since they know that the law wasn't made for us musicians, what's it matter? Several people are moving toward that flat, red disk which is the plain. They have one common destiny: the party. They walk hurriedly; no one wants to be the last. It takes almost an hour to get to the house. Next to the house is a stagnant lake from which rises the rank odor of something rotten. Some have arrived before us; they have to wait for our entry before going in.

As always, the door is closed; a gentle push and . . . it gives. Sixto, the drummer, is the first to take a seat. The old cripple and the one-eyed hag, preparing our drinks in a large tin, don't even bother to look at us. Over the first floating notes of my clarinet, the others follow and join in. Little by little, the house is filling up with people; as each one arrives, he pushes on the door, passes through, and closes it. The hosts, the old cripple and the hag, wait on us. The guests give the woman the gifts they have brought. The old cripple, serving each one in turn, passes around the drinks. We drink thirstily even though we know that the drink is made with water from the lake.

Those who arrive late don't come in yet; they look around to see who's missing, and when they see that some still haven't arrived, that they're not the last ones and that they, for tonight at least, are safe from the law, they breathe a sigh of relief and take their drinks. "So that it never happens to my son, I'll do the same for him that my father did for me: I'll make him a musician," says the cymbal player. The cripple and the hag laugh.

Don Belisano, who has just arrived, begs for another chance, "I didn't mean to be last. I've always been the one who—"

Now we all laugh. We laugh because someone is still missing, Don Seferino, the duck farmer, who arrives just at that moment. He realizes, on the spot, that he is last. He explains in shouts that he's not to blame, that the ducks which were his gift had gotten away from him and he'd had to chase them around the plain. There is total silence. The hag grabs the ducks away from him and the old cripple pats him on the shoulder. "Have your drink, don."

Now, Don Seferino has to dance with the hag. He dances until he's ready to fall down, but the old woman compels him to stay on his feet and follow the rhythm of the music, "Fly little pigeon, fly home to your nest," which the old cripple plays on my clarinet.

So it goes on every night. When the pair have finished the dance, the old man gives me back my clarinet. I have to keep on playing until dawn. Then the old man says, "The drinks are drunk up, gentlemen," and so we know it's time to leave. The last to arrive has to be the first to leave.

"It's daybreak, Don Seferino."

"No, please," sobs the old man.

But the law is the law. Don Seferino is pushed toward the door. The cripple gives the final push. Everyone, guests and musicians, watches through the window panes. Don Seferino beats on the door and begs them to open it. His voice grows weaker and weaker. Now we see him walk toward the stagnant lake and he disappears.

"We'll expect you all back tonight," says the woman as she opens the door.

THE FALL

Oscar Barbery Justiniano

"Are you in pain, brother?" He asked it softly, almost sweetly. The tone of voice struck a deep cord in Hernando and took him in.

"Yes," he answered, and his eyes filled with tears.

"I understand." The man spoke with conviction. "It's natural," he added thoughtfully. "Every human being has to suffer. It's in Genesis."

Despite the pain, the terrible sense of defeat, and his exasperating immobility, Hernando was interested. "Genesis?"

"Yes. The Genesis of man: 'In sorrow thou shalt bring forth children,' and 'In the sweat of thy brow shalt thou eat bread.' It's about pain, the reason why man is on this earth, as his punishment or his expiation. It also suggests our instinct for survival. First, man is born, next he's just hanging on to life. 'Thou shalt eat bread,' it says, 'by tearing it from the earth, snatching it from the beasts, fighting over it with other men.' And each time, as life gets more complex and difficult, the struggle gets harder, often cruel. The aggressors triumph; the passive and the meek perish. The pain you feel today, dear friend, is no more than a consequence of this pattern. You struggle for political power in this poor, backward country, with no work and little chance for improvement, and what you're really struggling for is bread. But the bakery's in our hands, and we'll defend it against everyone, God or the Devil. You understand me, dear friend?"

Hernando didn't answer. He was disgusted, and he wanted to throw up. He turned his face away. His hands and feet were asleep from the knots. But that wasn't what bothered him.

"This is a violent country," the man continued. "Some are violent on the attack; others on the defense. We have managed to get the better of our emotions. We can kill without anger when we decide it's necessary. Meanwhile, we have observed that aggression triumphs. Rats, when they can't find anything to eat, eat one another. As for people, the strongest and most ambitious go into politics. They can't just settle into the peaceful routine of some liberal political stance. They need wider horizons, because their work hasn't yet consumed them . . . it hasn't brutalized them. We understand. From somewhere deep inside, Nietzsche's will to power orders each person to conquer his own portion of power. But not, my dear friend, that crap about class struggle or economic laws. I mean the man who wants to fulfill himself, who wants to regain his self-respect, who wants to recognize himself as his own admirable creation. Some of us have already done it, have already conquered. Others—you, for instance—because they don't know how to justify themselves, invent ideals and causes, gather disciples around themselves, and denounce us. Your egoism needs to dress in a certain style to express the egoism of others. But if the cards were on the table, you would all see each other for what you are, and without anybody left to bluff, the game would be stupid. Am I exaggerating, brother?"

"You disgust me," growled Hernando. "God! How much have they made you do for them? You've become their mouthpiece, a mouthpiece for the dirty—"

"Dirt is what all big words are based on."

"Go away! Go on! What you'll never understand is that dirt can be molded into virtue."

"Virtue is an emotion. It's a face on a medallion. We've already overcome that theological ambivalence: Good and Evil, Yes and No. We aren't deceived anymore. We can't keep on calling weakness *goodness,* incompetence *resignation.*"

"You disgust me."

"No, brother, don't exalt yourself. You're still reciting your Christian Marxist catechism. Just now I remembered that you once called me your conscience. And now you don't want to face me?"

"You dirty everything. You can't raise yourself, so you try to drag everything down to your level. And you use cynicism to do it. Leave me alone. Your cynicism is just a form of denial—of life and all its values."

"I'm sorry. I really am. I don't want to hurt you. Not for humanitarian reasons, as they say, but because I consider it unnecessary. We don't do anything without a purpose. We are the wave of the future, the embryo of those to come, who will people the earth."

"Go away."

"All right. I'm going," the man said, standing up. "But I'll say one thing more: Your kind spring up like mushrooms wherever people born to disappear are hungry. We want to save those people if we can, but they're too much in a hurry, and it's all your fault. Those speeches of yours stir up appetites and longings for things they would never have dreamed of, and every time, they get meaner and more rebellious. But we're going to hold on to power no matter what. Don't forget; up until now, we haven't applied rational, disciplined force on you. You'll be set free soon, but don't try any more revolutions. I would be sorry for you, brother. Do you believe me?"

"Sorry? Your sentimentality surprises me."

"I despise it myself. I've already told you we're not yet the men of the future. The musk of weakness and emotions still clings to us. We're still able, fortunately, to admire someone, even. . ."

Hernando looked hard at the man. A dim, late afternoon light filtered into the cell from a high window. Suddenly he pitied this man who had first been his childhood companion, later his closest friend, and now his torturer. Paralyzed by the ropes, lying in the corner where he had been flung, he felt infinitely superior to him. Suddenly it became clear to him. Without meaning to he had always lorded over Luis. And it had always surprised him when he realized he was doing it. Whenever he had laid down a new rule for some game, without even planning to, he had issued some command; whenever he had given some advice or stated some opinion, Luis, the man who now stood over him insulting him, had followed his lead, had unconsciously taken orders from him.

It was instinct in Luis, an instinctive submission to Hernando's easy-going superiority—which Hernando had never abused. Perhaps, Hernando suddenly suspected, Luis had never shaken it off. Aroused by his memories, he raised his head as high as he could and spoke quietly but firmly, "Luis, untie me."

Luis hesitated. The firm voice of his old friend came to him clearly from the mists of a past that had fallen asleep within him but was not altogether dead. He felt around in his back pockets and pulled out something from one of them.

"Untie me," Hernando repeated.

Then Luis obeyed. He bent down to his friend and with a pen knife cut the bonds. The scabs rubbed loose, and fresh, warm blood trickled from the wounds.

Hernando stood up, free, and looked at his friend. He felt strong, tall, proud. His eyes dominated Luis, who was insignificant, hardly a shadow in the dim light.

"Open the door for me." It was Hernando's voice, still calm.

Luis hesitated again, another instant. Then the door was opened out to a clear, cool night. Hernando took a deep breath, almost unaware of Luis. He looked out onto a stretch of grass and, about thirty yards off, a bright light fixed to the top of a post.

"I'm going," said Hernando "All I have to do is get past that wire. Good-bye. And thank you." And he walked out of the cell.

Luis didn't say anything. Up until this point, he had obeyed mechanically. His mind had been blank. He watched his friend go off with a firm step, upright and fearless. A shadow passed over his face, and he answered softly, sadly perhaps, "Good-bye."

By now Hernando had reached the wire. The post lamp shone on him as he groped around for something to grip the wire with. He had already started climbing when Luis pulled out the pistol and aimed. The shots stopped only when Hernando lay still on the grass.

THE GODFATHER

Ramon Rocha Monroy

I would say that, beginning with the Land Reform, the number one vehicle for social mobility has been the truck. The *campesinos* who brewed this *chicha* (taste it: still foamy, still sticky, with the sweet smell and taste of corn) keep one hope locked in their piggy banks—and they feed it, penny by penny—one hope: to come to the city and buy a little pickup truck, first for trips to their village or down to the valley, later, as the trucks get bigger, to La Paz or Santa Cruz, and at last, to Arica, Peru! But deep down what they all want is to shake the manure from their heels and leave the farms forever.

You won't believe this, but that's exactly what Don Vito did. He was born into this world wearing rubber-tire sandals, because, don't forget, his mother wore a *pollera.* What? Those wrap-around, wool Indian skirts. See? There's one. There's another. Not that Don Vito ever farmed. Oh, when there was nobody else around to do it, he'd pick up a hoe. But his father had too much clout in the village for Don Vito to do much of that kind of work. The father had been a Liberal congressman, and President Ismael Montes was godfather to Don Vito, which made the two old men compadres; but when the time came, the old man forgot about the party, except for a note now and then to Don Ismael. That was because, as they say, the village has its charms.

You want proof? Every village anniversary the old man would make the same damn speech. "The fortress of La Colina," he'd proclaim, "and its proximity to Incallajta bear witness that this valley was a prominent vacation spot for the Incas. Centuries later, Goyeneche wrote in the *Kewinal* about the last disaster of Estaban Arze, that 'Bolivar if he had only had Bolivar's luck.'" You see the kind of Demosthenes the old man was! "This is the first reference," he would thunder, "to our La Coronilla!" Once he was warmed up, he would risk the wildest metaphors: "It is *our* harvests that break the demand for potatoes. Today, trains of mules, link by link, weave a network of transportation from La Coronilla to Cochabamba. The traffic is so thick it grinds to a halt, and it is not uncommon to see, in the heat of midday, loads of potatoes popping off the immobile backs of mules."

That was the village then; they say that only one souvenir survives from that era: this *chicha.* I can imagine the old man bragging about "our harvests"—as if he ever owned a patch of land. Not him, he was corregidor until he died (or I should say, honorary judge and mayor, since he didn't have a salary), and all he saved his money for was to go on splurges. But his wife, who was young and good looking and who probably had more to do with his staying than the attractions of the valley, was satisfied with the little under-the-table payments the judge received for his justice. Besides, there was never any lack of *chicha,* and their only expense was an occasional case of cheap snuff or Capstan cigarettes.

By the time the old man died, the main highway to Santa Cruz had bypassed the village, and the respectable people who still held onto their houses saw the streets more and more crammed with Indians. When the Land Reform came, there were *campesino* uprisings, and more crowds flooded in from the countryside. By the time the old man died, Don Vito's mother could see that things were looking up for her. She's still alive, she still lives in the village, and she still wears the *pollera.* But saying she still wears the *pollera* doesn't mean much. Who needs to wear a dress in a society of *polleras*?

By the time the old man died, Don Vito was already married to the woman who's his wife today. Look at her over there. Will you look at those brooches and rings, that peacock strut. Look at her showing off the silverware, bringing out the fancy china, making toasts with her new crystal. But deep down don't tell me you haven't noticed she's itching to eat with her fingers . . . like you and me, right? After all, the nobility eat with their fingers. Do you know how much that *pollera* cost? No, don't even guess. You couldn't. But why shouldn't she have it? When the old man died, she and Don Vito were working like dogs, selling potatoes at the country fairs. They had good times and bad times together. First they lived on a little beef jerky and field corn and worked with rented mules. Then they were tempted by city goods: mirrors, shoes, the first transistor radios. But they didn't give in to the temptations; they were too dedicated to fattening their purse, which was soon the size of a small pickup truck—a modest, second-hand, crank-start Chevy with a rebuilt engine that caught fire once when he was up in the hills driving around by himself. If he comes this way, you'll be able to see the scars on his hands. Something heroic in his trying to save the truck, don't you think? Bourgeois heroism, to be sure, the courage of a merchant protecting his merchandise, but still heroism, don't you think? No? Well, frankly, neither do I. Anyway, they bought another one, and another one after that, and still more . . . *trucks* I mean, each one bigger than the one before, trucks that inevitably moved them into the city.

First are the kids: the young lady, who is probably helping in the kitchen now, and the twin princes, the ones you see at the head table, carefree, elegant, good-looking guys. What did you say? No, of course not. Oh, sometimes they go there on holidays, but to actually move back to Don Vito's village, if you could even call it *move back* after so many years out in the world, growing up in the city here in this very house, them and their little sister . . . definitely not. As I told you, first the children came to board in the house of a friend of Don Vito's, who was actually the twin princes' tutor—I'll point him out to you in a minute—then more harvest and they had their own tiny house here, then a real house in the city, the same one where you and I—Go ahead! Help yourself; don't mind me. The point is Don Vito went through every mode of transportation. There are some who have even seen him plodding along like a burro with goods piled on his back—all for business. And he never left off selling potatoes.

Today you see him celebrating the homecoming of his sons and their birthdays and the New Year all by happy coincidence on the same day. Sure, today he's celebrating, but tomorrow he'll go out to the fields again. Not that he farms! Of course not! You see, he's so sly he puts even the Land Reform Law to work for him. Through the company? Yes, the company contracts—you don't have to tell *me* how they work. That's why he doesn't give a hoot about owning land. Before, the farmers had too much to do: growing crops, carting them into town, and selling them. Why sell them cheap in the village, he told them, when just a few miles further off I can get you triple the price? But don't think Don Vito speaks well of the Land Reform. He complains louder than anyone. I suppose he's forgotten when he was poor. Like today's importers, eh? They're the ones who scream loudest against the government, which provides them with quotas and coupons and loopholes.

Am I with the government? Don't make me laugh! They've even thrown me in jail, lots of times. But it's one thing for people like me to complain; on the other hand, these guys on the receiving end, I say they ought to keep their mouths shut. Don't you agree? And I say the same thing, and repeat it, about Don Vito. He's no Indian, absolutely not. You could even say he has the soul of an industrialist, or at least a foreman, surely. Well, to be more accurate, what he's got is the soul and smell of a peddler, especially the smell. If I only told you . . . he comes straight out of the country, but that doesn't keep him from despising country people. What? Dumb Indians? No, nobody says that anymore. Can anybody hear us? *Huayrapamushcas.* Today that translates as *he who is gone with the wind.* But what isn't gone is prejudice, racial slurs, patronizing.

Why patronizing? Because Don Vito is the *padrino.* He's the godfather of his own *compadres,* the baptismal *padre* of generations. Why? Who else is going to baptize a godchild's child? And if there's a wedding, who's going to give the bride away? And sometimes, as you seem to be implying, perhaps he's not only the baptismal father but the biological father as well. Tight, very apropos: "He who does not sleep with his *compadre* is homosexual," as they say. Here, look around you, they're all godchildren. The band leader's a godson. Another godson brought the *chicha.* Another one brought the lamb; another, the chickens; another, the squab. And tomorrow they'll slaughter a calf, brought by another. Don't worry, this will go on for at least a week. There's food and drink and no lack of help. That duck you're helping yourself to—Don Vito's wife prepared it. She's in charge of the kitchen, believe me, and she doesn't like to leave it. There was an army of goddaughters here yesterday, willing to cook, but all they got to do was help out. The final touches are hers. She'll be at it all week, and so will the goddaughters. Four of them will start each keg: one opening it, one skimming off the foam, one biting the siphon, and one bringing the pitchers. And four others will help: one washing the glasses, one drying them, one filling them, and one putting them on the trays. And serving *chicha* to us we have four times four!

The gifts are all, of course, from the country godchildren. But there are godchildren and *compadres* who live in the city, too, for example, that little school teacher standing over there, stiff as a brick wall mortared with *chicha.* Or over there, another teacher, *from* the country, of course. The only way to get out of the country is with your own truck or a teaching certificate. And look over there at Quinteros, who owns the funeral home, the one preoccupied with his new shoes; and look at Manapuede, next to him, the night watchman at the morgue, from Don Vito's village—another godson. Look at all of them, gawking at the twin princes' waltz. All of them, godchildren and *compadres,* are spellbound, except that gentleman —How shall I describe him?—the one with the broad forehead and the Bourbon nose, robust as a bishop, the eldest *compadre,* and the twin princes' tutor. Look at him wrinkling his nose to keep from laughing. Like you and me, eh? His little eyes twinkle, his cheeks twitch like a bunny's, and his arms hang akimbo like a monsignor's. Yes! That's what he likes to be called. Watch. Hello, Monsignor! See him smiling at me? Impressive, isn't he?

Who? The ones that are dancing, yes, they are the twin princes. Of course, they've graduated with professional careers. Here? Are you kidding? No. Abroad, far away from here. And now they're celebrating, both of them, by happy coincidence, their graduation, their birthday, and the New Year. Look at them, dressed up like princes and taking turns waltzing with their mother. Ah, but don't think just because she wears a *pollera* she's a *campesina.* Absolutely not—every morning she puts on French perfume, and she never dresses with less than five yards of the finest fabric. Well, yes, I agree; the *cueca* would have been a better dance, or at least more fitting. Naturally . . . since a *pollera* can't fall as elegantly as, say, a chiffon gown, and, I admit, the mother doesn't dance with quite the grace of her royal sons. But none of that matters as long as the godchildren are all gathered around gawking at them like frogs.

Listen to the applause, and we better not neglect to applaud too: Don Vito's looking this way. We were the only ones talking during the dance. Clap, and don't make fun of the princes' solemn faces: a prince inspires greater respect with a frown. This isn't courtesy, it's tribute, and even we are paying our dues—like at their high school graduation, remember? You don't? You know what it's like in the best school in the city, don't you? Well, at graduation they walked up onto the stage arm in arm with their mother. Mama mia, what a *pollera*! Sitting next to me a little old man, one of Don Esteban

Arze's descendants, no doubt, murmured, "My hands ache from clapping for those boys. What respect, what motherly pride." He wasn't mistaken, except that I would say *satanic* pride—these people who buy themselves seats in the temple of the aristocracy.

What aristocracy? I see what you mean. Nevertheless, before the Land Reform . . . do you realize that at the turn of the century *polleras* were forbidden on the public squares? Absurd, I know, but that absurdity endured until the Land Reform. Imagine, in a country of four million *polleras,* less than a million women could come into the public squares. As you say, though, the problem wasn't turning the pancake, but getting it right on both sides. And of course, it wasn't right for everybody. Take Don Vito's company: He monopolizes the potato crop in the village and in all the neighboring valleys. The farmers are all his godchildren, or his *compadres* or his children. Who knows? They work the land, and Don Vito provides the seed, fertilizer, insecticide; he personally oversees the plowing, the disking, the planting, the spraying, the harvest, especially the harvest. Exactly right—when the owner looks on, his horses grow strong—very appropriate. Oh, but don't think that with synthetic fertilizers and insecticides we now have efficient farming: I defy you to find one tractor in the whole region. Nothing but oxen, believe me, and, as I read somewhere, if the land belongs to those who work it, we should give it to the oxen. In Mexico—Have you been to Mexico?—In Mexico you could say that the land already belongs to the oxen, but now that they own it, they still work it for people.

Of the whole harvest, half goes to Don Vito, and the other half he buys cheap from his godchildren. Then he travels around night and day selling his product, which isn't bad product, as you can tell . . . but with all synthetic fertilizers, don't you think it's lost some of the flavor of the native potato? And if you only knew the route he travels. Even the snakes can't crawl it. The river road, for instance— the flood washes rocks onto it, and no one bothers to remove them. Then once you've crossed the river, you have to turn sharp to the left and climb for a mile and a half with your brakes wet. Your motor stalls, and down you go!

The next *cueca*? Certainly, Señora, thank you very much; just a few more words with this gentleman, and then we'll dance—very kind of you. No, the honor is mine.

This traditional native courtesy . . . as I was saying, it is a bad road. Of course, there's a little bridge now, but if it hadn't been for the priest—he raised the money back in his own country, and they're still blaming him for it here because it's too rickety, because it can't bear the truck traffic. Go ahead, ask me whose trucks! Think about this: if the road were good, how many other Don Vitos would be out there buying and selling potatoes? That's why it must be maintained exactly as it is, no better, no worse; and the same goes for the village. Why waste money that could be useful in the city? So the priest wants to build a church? Let him finance it the way he did the bridge. You know these foreigners. One day the priest realized that with a toll bar at one end of the bridge he could charge enough money for improvements. Understand? He figured he could collect almost a hundred thousand pesos in one year. But tell me, if you dare, whom he was going to collect that hundred thousand from. Don Vito, period, except for a few of his godsons. The toll bar didn't stand a chance! Same way with the mill—the priest thought it would be nice to give a mill to the village, if only anyone grew grain. So of course he started preaching that only grain could free the region from the yoke of the potato. Now we have a saying: the mill is for grinding water.

Another problem was the movie theater. Think of the unrest the educational films he brought back from his country could have stirred up among the *campesinos*! Don Vito, supported by the Neighborhood Civic Association, demanded a quick, private showing of the films. Then they accused the priest of the usual, and now the priest is celebrating mass back in his own country. And that was it. Protests? Some, especially from the *campesinos*. But their own leaders keep the troublemakers in line. And if the discontent grows, there's some little gift: ten thousand bricks, or something like that, which the *campesinos* themselves make when they could be working their land and which he buys from them at a discount. As they say, the straps come from the same hide.

But if that's the way Don Vito carries on up here, why, you ask me, do they respect him so much? Well, precisely because he is their godfather and *compadre*. Do you have any idea what bad luck it is to let a *compadre* down? Much less a godfather? The goddaughters know this better than anybody. If their husbands beat them or cheat on them or drink too much, they go running to Don Vito, and since he's the godfather, two roars from him is all it takes to set the husbands straight. As their godfather, he even has the right to whip them. Well, that's just an expression, I admit, because as far as I know the only whippings he's administered are tongue lashings, so far: "I'm going to horsewhip you, you little shit; don't think I won't. I'm your godfather, and I have the right!" Then you should see those godsons behave like little angels.

Besides, as I told you at first, every one of them is busy stuffing his money into a piggy bank. Of course, more give up halfway than actually save enough money for a pickup truck. Did I say piggy banks or under their mattresses? That was a lie. They bring it here, to this house, which serves as their bank; patiently, they deposit it, a hundred pesos at a time, all registered in a notebook a hundred pages long, with all the mistakes you'd expect anyway, which don't really disturb the *campesinos*. You see, these vulgar tricks are only incidental, because either he immediately lends the money out (at 4% monthly, of course) or, if worse comes to worse, puts it in a bank in the city, and even with the *annual* interest . . . well, sometimes all the capital goes into fertilizers, seed potatoes, insecticides, herbicides. That's when the game gets really interesting. If someone comes to withdraw his savings and Don Vito is in the country, he tells him, "Sure, just come back a little later. Then Don Vito hides in the city: he's in La Paz, he's gone to Santa Cruz, he's taken a load of potatoes to Arica. And when the godson gets over this hurdle, he meets even stiffer objections. If there's something wrong with the figures, it's because the account is too small: "How do you expect to buy a truck with 200,000 pesos, boy?" "But I believe there's already 300,000, Godfather." "Or with 300,000! We're talking about trucks. You think you just pick them up off the street?" But sure, some get over that hurdle, too. And then Don Vito goes and finds a pickup truck and gives it to the godson, who has been sleeping on his doorstep, eating at his table, and who has deposited all his money with him for that one purpose. And of course, there's a sales commission of five or ten thousand pesos, which the godson doesn't know about. After that there is driver training: *campesinos* don't know how to drive.

Meanwhile, Don Vito drives the poor truck to death, hauling potatoes all over the mountains for his own profit. And whether they learn to drive or not, I draw up a contract whereby they have to hire out the truck to haul his harvest at a fixed rate for, say, ten years. But, you ask me, what's the contract for? In the first place, when I say "Don Vito's trucks," I should specify that he only owns one; the rest belong to his godchildren. In the second place, if he weren't monopolizing them during harvest, the godsons might be tempted to go into business, too. As things are, they usually limit their hauling to their own harvests. Finally, of course, if there's anything left of the truck, if he's made anything off his land, and a bunch of other *if's,* you finally see the godson in the city with an insatiable appetite for new things and a truck festooned with geegaws. So, you might say, Don Vito uses other people's lands, hands, vehicles, and money (deposited at his house). Understand?

I don't remember if I told you, but I take care of all the legal matters. Don Vito brings them personally to me; otherwise the god-sons wouldn't even give me the time of day. They are mostly abstracts of title. Would you believe it, we celebrated the silver anniversary of the Land Reform in '77, and there are still people who haven't registered their deeds. There are people who don't work with Don Vito and who want to protect their claim. Suddenly they're threatened with eviction, and they don't have anyone to run to. With the same typewriter, I draw up the notices of eviction and the restraining orders. Don Vito leases their lands at four or five thousand pesos for ten years. All this, you understand, to insure that he has first claim on any contractual arrangements they enter into. I've drawn up hundreds of contracts, all sealed with the callused thumbs of *campesinos.* Recently somebody died without having registered his title deed; Don Vito turned the matter over to me, and what do you think happened? One day a *campesino* came to me, the eldest of the heirs. He told me not to worry with the title, because Don Vito was the only one who cared to mess with it. As for him, he didn't want to be tied to the land; he was coming to the city to work as a truck driver. Smart kid, as a matter of fact. But not all of them are like him. Most want to own land. Nothing tickles them more than a deed full of signatures, where someone reads them their name and their rights over their own little potato patch.

If you only knew how much we've earned drawing up deeds. You see that gentleman over there? The skinny one. Yes, the one who stopped the orchestra so he could play the concertina. He's the judge. What? Yes, he's another one of Don Vito's *compadres.* What? Well, actually, yes, Don Vito is my eldest son's godfather. As I said, we're all *compadres* here. But if I could tell you all the deeds we registered and the titles we transferred. Picture a whole week of handing them out, with a hired orchestra, seven cartloads of *chicha,* cows, sheep, pigs, chickens, ducks, pigeons. We set up a table in the village square behind the church and pulled title deeds one by one out of a suitcase, calling each *campesino* by name. Each one paid five hundred pesos, so that by the end of the week the suitcase was out of deeds and full of money. That was only in the mornings. In the afternoons there was one long party that moved from homestead to homestead to the tune of incessant *challacu,* with Slim over there playing the concertino and yours truly walking arm in arm with two local girls.

At the end of the week, we divided the money into two huge piles that we stuffed into sacks. And you should have seen the truck we used to bring back all the animals they gave us. This is no exaggeration: for the next six months all my wife did was slaughter animals. Ugh. It was enough almost to make me a vegetarian. Don Vito? Well, I believe he did get his initial commission—I'm not sure—but he didn't ask a cent from us. It doesn't usually go that way, you can be sure of that. Actually, I don't earn much—seriously. And besides, he does it to me sometimes, too. Remember the devaluation? I knew exactly when they were going to devalue, and I asked him to lend me fifty thousand pesos, to be returned in less than a week. Understand? He told me he didn't have a cent. But a month later, the little schoolteacher—the one mortared with *chicha*—said to me, "What a genius that Don Vito is. He changed fifty thousand pesos for dollars and almost doubled them." Did I say anything to Don Vito about it? Are you kidding? Besides, why should I have expected to be the exception? And there are rules even to exceptions.

What? Hmm, what a question. You want to know if he's happy? What about you? Are you happy? Me? Well, here, have a brandy. Here's to you. Look, every old guy looks back at his youth. If you had seen Don Vito, if you had heard him playing those folk tunes on the *charanga*—I can assure you that your local man is not happy. And if you don't believe me, wait till all this whooping it up dies down. If you can hang on with me until dawn, we'll pull out Don Vito's old *charanga* and you'll see. He doesn't weep, but it's worse. He sings with a broken voice, looking way off in the distance. No doubt he's remembering some of his first schemes, sometimes almost with nostalgia. I'm sure of that, because his type is vanishing. His daughters will marry well. They'll live well. They'll have beautiful children. The twin princes will forget the village, believe me. Oh yeah, they will keep stored in the cellar of their memory a few images of their village. But now the grandchildren, the great grandchildren . . . and don't worry; they'll all keep portraits of Don Vito and his wife in their living rooms, as if, how shall I say, as if they were the mythological founders of an empire. If you live long enough, you'll see her painting, of course.

That's why I'm telling you—the local traditions won't last. And deep down that saddens me. If you don't believe me, notice that the twin princes don't have half the godsons that Don Vito does. Their status comes entirely from the awe Don Vito inspires and from all the jostling to get on Don Vito's good side. See the way everyone's warming up to you suddenly. Do you notice the envy? They're looking at you. Understand? Notice how obsequiously they offer you that *tutuma*. Notice Don Vito smiling at you. And you aren't appreciating Don Vito's smile.

"They're smiling at you, too. This girl who's joined us . . . she looks like Don Vito."

"As a matter of fact, she's his daughter."

"Ah! His little girl! And is she single?"

"This is my wife."

THE LAST

Walter Montenegro

> *The last will be first, and the first last.*
> —MATTHEW 20:16.

In the tender, loving voice with which some mothers ask their children's forgiveness for having brought them into the world, his mother would say to him, "My son, the last will be first, and the first last. Our Lord has promised this, and we must ignore the troubles of our lives in this vale of tears, which is only a short wait before our eternal joy. True happiness is There, not here."

Juanito listened to these words without understanding them completely. When his mother said *There,* she raised her eyes toward the sky, and she lowered them to the floor when she said *here.* He figured there was surely more chance for happiness up than down. So why get too upset over his difficulties on the brick floor of this world? Difficulties such as the mean tricks other schoolchildren played, which didn't seem so unbearable, being simply problems whose happy solution waited for him There, on the blue chalkboard of the sky.

Life sometimes takes nasty turns. During his school years, the life Juanito Perez had to either struggle against or resign himself to found its most concrete form in Nicomedes Galvan, dressed, despite his huge size, in a sailor suit and shorts, terrorizing his classmates with his fat, brown fists. He was a master of the blow to the solar plexus that left his victim breathless and the hammer lock which he applied until stars went shooting off behind his victim's closed eyes.

"Who is your boss? Who is your boss?"

"You, Nico, you are my boss. Stop, stop . . ."

Then Nicomedes would smile with such satisfaction that even the pockmarks on his face seemed to be smiling, too.

Juanito Perez always shrank when he passed near the bully, anticipating the fist falling on the back of his neck or on his kidneys. When it did fall, he applied his secret formula like a magic ointment —"The first will be last . . ."—and he imagined Nicomedes Galvan in the next world (whether with wings is not certain) patiently tying

Juanito Perez's shoes or copying out his arithmetic for him. Not for one moment did it enter his mind to doubt the existence of shoes in heaven, or bald, inexorable arithmetic teachers.

Years passed. Juanito Perez turned into Juan Perez. He started signing his full name, Inocencio Juan Perez, as if to amplify his image in this world. His mother's bright and ingenuous aphorism was losing its luster. Life had scrubbed the shine off it with the bitter brush of poverty. Even his mother disappeared one day, depriving his spiritual vista of her sweet face that radiated resignation and otherworldly illusions.

There was a period when Inocencio Juan devoured all those books entitled *Will Power, Help Yourself,* etc. He practiced optimistic smiles and tried, with all the power of his eighteen years, to help not only himself but other people, too. His success matched the wrinkles of his badly-ironed pants better than the heroism of his efforts. His brave impulses were slowly dissolving under the drizzle of daily disappointments. He finally came to the conclusion, perhaps without even knowing it, that only on the other side of eternity would he receive the first prize that was due him for coming in last now. It would be fair to think that meanwhile, in the book of eternal justice, the name of Inocencio Juan Perez was beginning to figure among the names of the elect.

One day Inocencio Juan fell in love. No doubt she was one of those women who in times of war or flood would be taking in orphans and tending to the sick. She must have put a lot of herself into provoking the first date, because Inocencio Juan's methods of seduction were limited to furtive glances and long waits at the corner of her block—not the nearest corner, but the one farthest from her house.

Inocencio Juan fought valiantly to offset the ugliness and poverty in their romance with some touch of beauty, of poetry. By the expensive and short-lived light of love, he arrived thrilled and on time for their dates at the doorway of her house. When the neighborhood kids went by, making dirty remarks and suggestive gestures, he always blushed and stammered, "The weather's nice, fortunately." He would look up at the sky, and she would squeeze his arm in reply.

One winter day, escaping from the children's heckling, he and his sweetheart came to the public park at the poetic hour when twilight falls over the city. Through cold lips they had to force their words, punctuated by the chattering of their teeth. Often they had to repeat themselves to be understood. Their few frozen smiles and the little puffs of vapor issuing from their mouths made their meeting look sadly surreal.

She leant her head on his shoulder, and he felt an unfamiliar simmering through all his veins. He shut his eyes and suddenly realized that his hand was advancing up her arm to her shoulder, to her breast, with the fearful caution of a blind man on a strange street. His hand unbuttoned her collar, approached her flesh, and felt its warmth even before caressing it, but the cold of his fingers produced such a violent reaction that his anxious touch was immediately rebuffed. Little by little, Inocencio Juan lowered his hand, without daring to look. She rebuttoned her dress without saying a word.

Later, as arm in arm they left the park, passing dozens of cars parked in the shadows of the trees, Inocencio Juan coughed slightly, envying the animals who make love only in the spring and the men who make love in places where seasons don't exist.

Later came the obscure life of a poor husband: always the same clothes, never old enough to throw away; the inaccessible Christmas store windows; the same greasy, tasteless food every day; his wife's hands stained and knotty, nothing like the white, refined hands of the woman he had courted; the faded orange blossoms forgotten in a drawer; the bridal gown prudently cut up and tacked to the window for curtains; and Inocencio Juan's twelve shirts, bought before the wedding, "to keep for later," transformed into diapers for their son.

From there he went to the office, to endure the abuse of the first clerk, an elegant Don Juan who was always in a hurry, chatty and easygoing with his superiors, stern and strict with his underlings, whose frown commanded the humblest acquiescence to his demands of individual accountability for the most insignificant expenses. Inocencio Juan spent eight hours a day bent over the interminable white of the ledger, eight hours feeling the eyes of the first clerk, who sat behind him, slipping distastefully over his neck, as if surveying slum garbage.

There was a period when Inocencio Juan would have hated the first clerk, if he had known how. That was after the death of their son. When the boy fell sick, the doctor prescribed a "change of climate," the brilliant counsel of medical science after thirty centuries of progress. And Inocencio Juan crouched on his work stool day after day, waiting for a breach in the barbwire fence of the first clerk's severity that would allow him to ask for an advance in pay. But he was so timid and let so many days go by without articulating his request that the climate changed on its own, and the child went on a permanent voyage, to breathe the salutary air of eternity. The only mementos the child left behind were a few diapers and a stubborn, silent grief, like winter rains, in the eyes of his mother.

At last one day the eyes of the first clerk slipped past Inocencio Juan's neck without frightening him. But why now, Inocencio Juan asked himself. His sense of his duty as an underling was disturbed. I'm losing my grip, he thought. I'm not myself. But not even these thoughts could convince him to get a hold of himself. Worse, the ledger sheet seemed like a quiet white invitation to do nothing. Inocencio Juan gazed at it without the least desire to soil it with his now somewhat shaky handwriting. A strange chill was beginning to settle over everything, including his enthusiasm for his duties as a second clerk.

Undoubtedly it was a day for extraordinary events, because the supervisor, the inexorable supervisor whose glasses enlarged his accusatory eyes, did not utter his customary reproaches, which invariably ended, "Nobody knows how to work here; when I was in London . . ." No, nothing like that. Instead, he took a long look at his miserable underling, hunched like a yellow worm over the ledger, and he spoke to him the strangest sentence that Inocencio Juan, in his twenty-five years of experience, had ever heard, "Go on home and rest today and tomorrow. You're sick."

"But sir, I don't . . . I . . . I don't think I've done anything to make you—"

"No. That's not what I'm saying. You go to bed. A supervisor must be understanding with his underlings." And he expatiated on how underlings should be treated.

Inocencio Juan didn't get to hear the whole lucid discourse because when he stood up from his work stool he collapsed, as if from the sudden rupture of the umbilical cord that held him to his ledger. As he came to himself, he grasped weakly for the eraser, as if he wanted to erase the mark this slip of his had made on his previously unblemished record, but he found himself being pushed toward the door, his hat inexplicably crowning his head and weighing down on it like a rock.

"Shall I call a car?" the quick-witted office messenger asked the first clerk, who was still contemplating Inocencio Juan's departure with his usual air of superiority.

"No, no. Back to work, mind your own business, boy. A little walk will do him good. When I was in London. . ."

Inocencio Juan still had enough strength to smile gratefully from the door. As he dragged his feet along the sidewalk, he vaguely wondered if having ever been to London might have made it possible for him to lean back now into the soft seat of a car, like the one on their wedding day, between the church and home. The air seemed full of the ringing of bells and sweet memories of his courtship with Dorotea; that tall, stiff collar that he had had so much trouble unbuttoning; the wedding and the congratulations, while a small band kept playing, first the wedding march, then dragging on until finishing with a few sad tangos. Everybody had congratulated him, and Inocencio Juan had invariably answered with the same phrase, shaking flabby, cold, hard, hot, rough, and mostly damp hands. When a waiter came up to offer him a glass of beer, Inocencio Juan had repeated his usual, "A thousand thanks," and mechanically reached out his hand, but the waiter didn't take it.

Full of these thoughts and with a faint smile on his lips, he arrived home. Dorotea let out a cry as soon as she saw him. What must he look like to produce such strange responses in people?

He was so used to nobody bothering with him, like old clothes that you wear and no one notices, that he was bewildered to find himself in bed, sick, and the object of his wife's and the neighbor women's attention. Suffocating from the heat that burned his lungs and throat, a biological terror took hold of him when he woke up late and wasn't at the office.

One day one of his office mates came to see him and told him how the first clerk had reprimanded the office workers, urging them to put their lives in order and not get sick, because sickness disrupts the work schedule and inconveniences the management, who, for their part, keep watch night and day to insure the well-being of their underlings. The first clerk had concluded his reprimand by citing the case of an employee who had failed shamefully in his responsibilities by getting sick at the very moment when his services were most needed in the office. "Because in London there are certain things which are not tolerated," the powerful clerk had concluded, putting special emphasis on the two words "certain things."

Inocencio Juan tried to pronounce some eloquent phrase for his friend to transmit to the supervisor, explaining that he wasn't in bed because he wanted to be there, but because of some incomprehensible plot between his wife and the doctor, and that he would soon be back at work. But he couldn't say much for lack of breath, and besides, the look in his office mate's eyes really alarmed him; he kept quiet and decided that something strange was happening to everyone who came near him.

The priest's visit and the last rites (safe conduct to happiness) were what let him in on the big secret: he was dying. He was suddenly terrified, unable to think with the philosophical detachment of whoever had said, "Death is just one more adventure, where all we lose is a cadaver." In the first place, he could not forget that, in addition to his own, he would leave behind the almost-cadaver of his wife. Secondly, as we already know, for him death would be the only noteworthy adventure he had had in life.

Invaded by hundreds of thoughts, he did not pay strict attention to the priest, whose questions were getting more and more complicated and accusing—absurd, I should say, because what point could there be in asking a second clerk questions like, "Have you coveted your neighbor's wife?" "Have you wished for your enemies' deaths?" What enemies? And who would a second clerk's neighbor's wife be? And what is *fornicate*? The odd words these priests use!

Disconcerted, Inocencio Juan confessed a thousand sins. He said yes and no at random, because what really frightened him about death was the unpaid rent, what would happen to his wife, even the last unchecked figures he had left on the ledger, but, no, not by any means, not all this incomprehensible business of neighbor's wives and fornicating. But now the priest pardoned everything, because after all, priests are more inconvenient than bad. They always pardon, first clerks as well as second.

Inocencio Juan called anxiously to his wife. She approached the bed, her eyes red with sleeplessness and sobbing. She took his hand, something she never did; this romantic business of holding hands is for people with nothing else to do and people on their death beds.

"Dorotea, I'm dying."

"Don't say that, Juan. You're better. You'll be well soon . . ." Her sobs wouldn't let her finish.

"I tell you, I'm dying. Didn't you see the priest? Priests only come when you're dying."

"Don't talk that way, Juan. Not now that you're clean of sin."

"Dorotea, forget about sins and listen to me. They owe me a half month's pay at the office. Also—"

"Don't tire yourself. Talking's bad for you."

"Dorotea, ask someone about the pension fund. I think it has to do with widows of employees."

The word *widow* upset her terribly.

"Dorotea . . ."

He couldn't say more. His voice stayed stuck in his throat. Only a disagreeable hiss escaped through his lips, reinforced by a chorus of sobs around the room, as he approached that huge edge from which first and second clerks make the same definitive leap toward nothing. Suddenly into his memory flashed the theme of his miserable life, that consolation stuck in the bottom of his spirit, like a cork in the hull of a boat. He saw his mother leaning over his bed, reciting one more time, "My son, last will be first, first, FIRST, FIRST." The word kept repeating, larger and larger, pulling him into an infinite whirl.

And he died, and went, we may be certain, to assume a post of great responsibility in the management of the no doubt complicated account books of Heaven.

THE RETURN

Renato Prado Oropeza

The man looked to the right and to the left of the station—not one person. The noise of the train faded away behind him. His own footsteps sounded loud but uncertain, like the sound of a bottle rolling down steps. Nobody.

The man looked at his shadow. He didn't know what to call this creature that stuck close to him in the world of light and dust—because just "my shadow" reduced it to the category of *thing,* like saying "my shoe" or "my shirt," and a person's shadow is more intimate, more personal. But he couldn't think of a better name before his shadow disappeared, first head, then body, and was lost in the dirty station lobby. "Nothing and nobody."

Now the man didn't even have his shadow. He put his suitcase on the floor. Nobody was in the building, either. "But who the hell's supposed to wait on you here?" he muttered.

It seemed like a bizarre dream, like one of those absurd delusions that occur when the mind breaks out of its bounds and tells itself, "Okay, let's rewrite history our way. Today it's going to happen like this: I'm sick of living in the city, in this crummy hotel room, living like a stranger among people who jostle me on the buses and in the movie theaters. I'm sick of all that, and then I remember that I do have somebody out there, in my hometown, and it so happens that I want to see this somebody of mine. I pack my bags and here I am. I'm back . . ."

"I'm back," said the man.

A little dog, old and shaggy, emerged from a corner and came toward him, lifting his snout and sniffing the strange city smell. "Well, at least this mutt's here," said the man.

He walked out of the station and there was a boy, looking at him from an open window. It was a low window, and the boy was leaning over the sill, looking up and watching him, without moving. "Do you know who the station master is?" the man asked.

The boy didn't answer him and didn't take his eyes off him. A stream of saliva trickled down his chin and wet his chest. "Revolution," the idiot finally gurgled.

The man didn't catch the word. The sun dragged the man's shadow out into the open again. "Come on," he said to the dog, and turned the corner onto the first silent street.

The street was two or three blocks long and ended at the town square. The man remembered it perfectly. The only thing that had changed was the color of the houses. They were sadder and tireder from the daily wear of the sun and wind. The dog stopped and began whimpering. "Come on," said the man.

There was a shot. The dog scampered into the doorway of one of the houses. Through a crack in the door, the man could see the eyes of little children. They blinked and went out like sparks. "Hey!" called the man.

The door opened a bit, creaking. Three children watched him suspiciously. "I'm from this town, too," said the man.

"There's a revolution," said the oldest child. The man didn't say anything. "They want to punish the commissioner."

From the square, they could hear more shots.

"They say he's a very bad man."

"Papa went, too."

The man wanted to ask about Laura but decided that would be silly. The sun was wearing him down. The dog trotted through the door, sniffing the cracks in the wall. "It would be better inside," the man thought, and he took two steps into the hallway, trying to smile at the children, who, with one movement, stepped backward. But they didn't seem frightened.

"Are you from the city?" one of them asked, blushing.

"Yeah, sure," said the man.

"Then you've been to the movies," said the oldest child. The children's eyes were bright with excitement. The sound of gunshots continued in the square. The children didn't seem to be paying attention to anything except this stranger.

"I'm looking for someone," said the man.

"If you don't know which house it is, I can find it for you," said the oldest child.

"Laura's house," said the man. "You see, Laura used to live on the street that crosses the square."

The boy seemed to be thinking very hard. The man wanted to ask if he knew the house and if he knew Laura. The man was making a great effort to remember her face, but so many years had passed, and the city, with its bustle and its worries, had dispelled all traces of her image.

"Laura . . . Laura who?" asked the child.

The man wasn't paying attention. The shooting had gotten more intense, and some people were running down the street, shouting. "Laura who?" echoed mechanically in his brain—Laura, the woman who had never left the limits of this tiny village, the only woman who, was she still alive, might be able to speak his name with surprise, maybe affection. "I can find the house myself," he said.

Somebody called to the children from a room inside. "That's Mama," said the oldest child.

"Okay, good-bye then," said the man, and he picked up his suitcase.

"What about your dog?" asked one of the children.

The old dog was resting quietly with his muzzle on the floor. "Come on," the man said, but the animal didn't make a move to follow him.

As the man was going out, somebody came running past him toward the door and knocked him over. "Hey! What are you doing?" the man shouted. He would have liked to protest more energetically, since the person who had knocked him over didn't even turn to answer him, but a sudden burst of machine gun fire struck him in the chest. He felt a pleasant sensation of something warm entering his flesh, warm little insects moving their tiny legs in his veins.

One of the children ran out of the house and stared at the man. His face looked like a kewpie doll's: it was diffusing and losing its outlines. The man tried to stand up. He couldn't. He was flung down there in the middle of the deserted street. The sun pressed against his forehead, which was beginning to throb furiously. His blood pumped: "Laura who?" The child's face was now an enormous mass of fog, the same color as the yellow wall of the house, heavy and overwhelming, with a small hole that seemed to be asking him, "Laura who?" as the mass pressed against his glassy eyes.

OBEY THE LAW

Paz Padilla Osinaga

When I found out my third brother, Francisco, had died, I had no choice but to face my fate. Since he'd died like all the others, his death musta been the will o' God.

My first brother died in agony. I remember it well, as if it were yesterday. One day he come up with the idea that he was gonna die, 'cause he was bewitched. He said he'd read it in the coca leaves and that's how it come out. O' course, I didn't pay him no mind, it seemed like a lotta crap to me, so I just told 'im to shut up, that he was just gonna bring it on if he kept talkin' like that, and so it happened. Three days later he started havin' stomachaches and shakin'. He said it felt like somebody was squeezin' his guts. Emerency, that's his wife, said she'd give him a potion for it, but nothin' seemed to ease his pain. He kept on tossin' and turnin' like he was layin' on hot sand. He'd sweat buckets o' sweat, an' then he'd cool down a bit. Everybody that looked at him said he looked real bad.

On Friday, that awful day, he got worse, yellin' an' beggin' us not to leave him, that the devils was takin' him away.

Seein' him like that, we went to fetch Dona Damian, the healer, so she could take a look at 'im. She made some incense. Then while she massaged his body with alcohol and ointment, she started chanting three long chants. She asked for a pot of hot coals. She hung some broom straws over the hot coals so they would catch fire. When the ashes fell down into the ointment, they made strange figures that only she could read. She shook her head and said, "The devil's in charge of his soul now. He's gonna die; that's for sure."

He lasted one more night, until the cock's crowin' at dawn. During the night, he kept slippin' out and gettin' away. We'd try to stop him, but four men couldn't hold 'im down. But he'd never get far; he'd get to the outer gates and then he'd walk back, all stiff and zombie-like, askin' us to forgive him for everything. Just before he died, his pain seemed to subside, and he stopped tryin' to get away. He called all of us together. He asked pardon of all of us and to Medardo, the second brother, he gave the charge: "Since we don't have a daddy, it's up to you to look out for your younger brothers. An' since you don't have a wife, you're gonna hafta take mine and look after my little son. It's the law and God wills it."

He said that, and then he died.

The charge he left to me was the heaviest . . . one that would spread out over a long, long time: first watchin' all the others die, and then, waitin' for my turn . . .

Medardo was resigned to takin' the widow, but at least they were happy about it, and she found herself with child without waitin' even a year. All kinds o' rumors began spreadin' through the whole town. Some said the two of them had bewitched and poisoned Emerejildo so they could be together. Others said it wasn't showin' proper respect for the dead for her to get with child so soon. The rest just listened to the gossip and added their say-so.

Me, I didn't pay no mind to the rumors. There wasn't no evidence of them ever havin' feelings for each other while Emerejildo was alive. Why, some folks went so far as to say they'd loved each other since they were kids. They said Medardo was foolin' around with Emerency when she'd come by to leave the lunch for her daddy in the pasture. They'd meet under the *guañunas* trees at the banks of the river in secret whenever they could. When she'd go take the sheep to the pasture, Medardo would go out to meet her in the fields and sing her love songs in the pasture. An' sometimes, when Medardo was really desperate, he'd come out on the path where she was goin' down to the river, real late, to get water in her bucket. They'd fall down together in the beauty of the *guañunas* by the banks of the river.

O' course, without knowin' about any o' this, Emerejildo married her, and since he was the oldest brother, she went along with it. If he did know anything, he felt safe in the respect that was due him, for bein' the oldest. But the time would come for Medardo and Emerency to answer to God.

About that time the Camba gang came along. They came up from the prairie—there were about fifty and they were armed. But they said they were not bandits, they were a squadron, here to protect us from the Collas who were gathering in the high plains. They called for every man old enough to fight to help them defend our lands, our women, our animals, the honor of our dead. Since I wasn't old enough to fight yet, I didn't go. Medardo went with them. Some said it was his destiny to go lookin' for death because it was forewritten. Anyway, he had no regrets about goin' off and leavin' a son in Emerency's womb.

We heard that the Camba group faced the Collas in Charaguayco, and the fight was on. Bullets whistled past their ears and the men would dive into every nook and cranny to shield themselves. The bullets were falling like rain.

The combat went on for days. At the end of that time, there was a heap of bodies on both sides. The winners turned out to be the Cambas, and those that survived the battle escaped to the mountains. Some retreated as far as the cypress groves, and from there they took refuge in Valle Grande. Others cut loose on the road to San Juan, passing on from there to Palma Sola. Some came as far as our village, wanting to use it as a defense by making use of the big rocks that encircled our dwellings. Within the rock formation, where the village nestles, would be a perfect fortress from which to attack the Collas. But the villagers were afraid that the town would disappear into a combat zone, so they didn't let them stay.

Then the Collas came, and they possessed the town and told us they were here to defend us from the Cambas, so we had to feed and shelter them anyway, just as we'd done for the Cambas before.

Meanwhile, there was still no news of Medardo. People said that, probably having survived the fighting, he would have gone somewhere to forget what had happened. My mama thought that since he knew the land so well, he was surely hiding someplace, waiting for the last of the Collas to go away. But that was not the case. A man living near where the fighting had been was unable to bear the thought of all the unburied bodies of the dead from both gangs. He began to despair at seeing his dogs go out early in the morning to feed on human flesh, returning at nightfall with their gorged bellies dragging the ground. Well, this man took pity on the dead and decided it was his duty to give them Christian burials as best he could. This man told us about Medardo. He said he'd found one that looked like Medardo, and he'd buried him in plain sight, so that his son could come fetch us. We went to see, we dug him up, and yes, it was him. We brought his body back to the village to bury him at the cemetery like a Christian should be, so we could save his soul from wanderin' eternally in search of peace.

Emerency was a widow for the second time, and now there were only two of us brothers left to fulfill the law, like it or not.

Well, that death didn't arouse suspicion because it was by chance that Medardo got killed, but Francisco, the third one of my brothers, began to have fears that death was waiting for him also. My mama intervened to convince 'im: "The Law orders us to stay united and protect each other. You have to obey the Law. If you break the Law, even God will forsake us."

Francisco, in spite of the fact that he had his life all planned out and was about to marry a woman in Pacay, had to take the widow and be resigned to it. Besides that, he had to care for the widow's two children, 'cause they were his own nephews and he had no reason not to want 'em.

When people are idle, they look for work for their tongues to do. It just goes to show you, 'cause now they began to blabber about the life of poor Francisco. They would have it that he wouldn't last more'n a year, that the widow woman was surely some kind of witch or somethin'. From that and other stories came bigger rumors. Some said the end of the world was comin', and these were the signs—a test to see if everybody was obeyin' the Law. Others said that it was a demon thing because ever since Father Cabot had come and burst the devil into three pieces in the village square, Pampa Grande had smelled like living hell for two months and every family who'd seen it couldn't think of anything but obeying the Law.

Then priest Apolinar came along and said that all of that stuff was pure devil wives' tales and that we had better do something about it before God should decide to punish us for conniving with a messenger of Lucifer. But while they was plannin' what to do, well, along came another death.

They found Francisco on the riverbank, face down beside a pool. At first the townspeople believed that the death had somethin' to do with the plague that had come into the village a few days before. Cows, horses, donkeys, goats, sheep, and even pigs were comin' down with fevers, and if one of them should drink the water, it would die, right off. The cows would come down from the highest mountain peaks and drink the river water, and then they'd die on the banks of the river. Francisco looked as if he'd been drinking water from the pool.

His wife said he'd been good and healthy, that he'd just that day been to Don Flores' pasture to borrow a yoke for his oxen so he could get his fields ready before the first rains. She also said that he'd not been showin' any signs of wantin' to die because she hadn't heard his soul followin' him around at night, and it wasn't as if she was a light sleeper, 'cause the house was always quiet. When a soul follows a body around, it retraces the steps during the night of all the things that body did durin' the day, an' it always does this if a body is goin' to die. The soul retraces its steps for weeks and comes closer and closer near the day of death, until it reaches the person. This didn't happen with Francisco; he died with no warning.

Well, it only took Emerency sayin' that for people's tongues to start waggin'. They said Francisco's death, bein' without warnin', wasn't a natural death—so they accused her o' bein' death in person and said that she was carryin' off the souls of the people of Pampa Grande before their time. Because of that, they took Francisco's body to the church to keep watch over it so the devil wouldn't get his soul. Everybody took turns keepin' watch all night so Lucifer and his angels wouldn't get what wasn't rightfully theirs.

I can't begin to tell you how I felt when Francisco, the third of my brothers, died, with me being the next one in line to the widow and her three sons, my nephews—this being my inheritance. A few days before my brother died, I was on the brink of goin' over to Tembladera to get myself a woman and marry her, to save myself from the possibility of receivin' the responsibility of Emerency, but I just didn't have the courage—if it hadn't been for fear of the Law. I believe that it was what my mama told me that convinced me to wait. " I have dreamed that Destiny is saving that woman for you," she told me. "I don't know why God didn't make you my first son, and then perhaps your brothers would not have had to die . . ."

I had no choice but to take the burden of death on my shoulders, and go on living with the waiting, waiting for the hour when I, too, should render my soul unto God.

THREE RAINS

Blanca Elena Paz

I search my memory and find you, Luz Marina, sitting at the edge of my bed in our room in La Plata. You have just touched my shoulder and awakened me, and into my ear you say, "You hear the rain? Let's go for a walk."

We went for lots of walks, Luz Marina, in the rain or in the sun. Those were our best years, our college years. It wasn't just the room we shared, but dreams, boredom, hunger. And sometimes, when your check or mine arrived, pizza and a bottle of wine!

I still haven't lost the image of the rain bouncing off your blue umbrella. I can still hear the noise of your footsteps on the lilac carpet of the park. The lilac color, Luz Marina, that only flowers that fall from the jacaranda tree have.

There you are, in my memory, in your white coat, working with your small, skillful hands at the hospital. And we're together on the beach, looking out at the ocean. We don't mind that there's nothing but two *salchichas* left for us to eat. I can see the plaza, the orange trees, the fountain, and the cathedral. My memories are filled with the smells of magnolias and linden trees. Sitting on a bench, you and I chatter on like two parrots. So what if our boyfriends have left us; something better'll come along. So you get angry; I'll wait and you'll get over it. So I'm in a bad mood; I'll get over that, too, and then we'll have a good laugh—laughter that I can't hold onto, just like the images. We aren't in the same room anymore, or the same city. You went back to your country; I to mine.

I didn't try to write you when I read the news in the papers. I just told myself it couldn't be real. But then it was shown on television. The events really had happened. But there was still one fact I knew about you that I latched onto: you were restless and could never stay in one place too long, so I wrote your brother in Bogota, asking about you. Today, after a long wait, I got the answer. Know what I did? I rummaged up the New Year's card your mother sent me three years ago. It was with the poncho and the little doll and the other things you'd given me. I looked at it for a long time as if time had come to a stop in it, as if trying to find you in it.

It's raining this afternoon, and I'm going out for a walk. Tomorrow's Christmas. Now, walking in the rain, I think about you. Now it doesn't make any difference whether the rain is here or there. My vision is blurred, and I think you're with me. The rain streams down my hair and forehead and mixes with the rain from my eyes.

"You hear the rain? Let's go for a walk."

And I picture you, Luz Marina, running through the streets of Armero, in a rain of bullets.

THE LIGHT

Blanca Elena Paz

You're worried. Your husband has changed a lot in the past few months. It isn't that he's stopped loving you. Actually, he's never been so tender. It's just that at certain moments you notice that he's distant, off somewhere else. Now that you really think about it, the day he began to change was when that woman came looking for him, the one who was pregnant. Another doctor had come to relieve him, and he was just about to go off duty when she showed up. She burst out crying when she saw him and fell on her knees. And, well, you know how your husband is. He let himself be talked into something. It was about a man with a bullet wound. Your husband extracted the bullet, stitched up the wound, and did not fill out a report for the authorities.

After that, even though he didn't tell you, you knew the woman had come looking for him again. Yes, that was the day. That was when he started changing. Some days he comes home so tired he doesn't want to do anything but sleep. And you can't sleep unless you read some first. You leave the bed-table lamp off until he goes to sleep. Then you read. Since the curfew went into effect, the nights have been long and tedious. The television is unbearable, just westerns and military reports, so you turn it off. Well, at least you've still got that right: if they censor you, then you'll censor them!

Late into the night, when the hands of the clock are marching toward morning, the city becomes filled with a weird and menacing orchestra. Trucks patrolling, breaks squealing, tommy guns rattling, boots . . . and you know, though you don't want to talk about it, what's going on in the streets. You've wondered if your husband has had anything to do with this mess. No. He's never cared for politics; although it's possible, now that he's started changing . . . you yourself have been changing. He's asleep. Asleep. It's better not to think about things and sleep. Put out the light, sleep, and do not think about the noise of footsteps in the street—in your street.

You want to get up and look out through where the slat's missing in the Venetian blinds and see what's going on. No. Better not, because the boots are getting closer. The house next door? You think about the brass plate on your door, with the M.D. on it, as if that plate made your house inviolable. Yes, it's better to turn out the light and not know. After all . . . you . . . what can you do? You can't change the world. You throw up your hands because you've realized the boots are coming toward your house. Did you leave the door unlocked? No. But you feel it opening. Your left hand reaches toward your husband's body. With your right you fumble for the light switch. Someone on the other side of your bedroom door is turning the knob. And at last you put out the light because you realize, too late, that the only refuge left you is the dark.

SYMMETRY

Blanca Elena Paz

Omar, our brother, doesn't seem to see her. Mama passes by her without noticing her. Anyway, Alva is there. I look at her, I smile, and I keep quiet. When Mama or Omar catch me talking to Alva, they get mad. My mother has just taken the portrait of Papa down from the wall and leaves the house with Omar; they're going to have it reframed.

"Alva," I say to my sister, "do you think about Papa?"

"Yes, Aurora, I think about him."

I remember that on the night Papa died, we were forbidden to come out of our room. We were afraid. We began to cry. Then Papa came to see us. He said he had to make a long journey. When we told Mama that Papa had come to say good-bye to us, she got very angry.

"Alva, Papa would never have doubted me."

"No, Aurora."

When Granny died, it was the same thing: They shut us up in our room and told us not to come out. Alva suggested we slip out the window, and that's what we did. Granny was in the garden, knitting in the darkness.

"I don't need lights to knit," she said, and gave us a kiss. She said she was knitting a shawl because she had to go on a trip.

"Granny's going on a trip!" we burst out, shouting in unison in the parlor. And then we got quiet, because Granny, among the flowers and the candelabra, was in her coffin sleeping.

"Alva," I give her the sign to be quiet, " it looks like Mama has changed her mind about going to the picture framers."

Mama climbs up the stairs. I hear the noise of her footsteps. I go to the window and look out. Omar is in the car. He's trying to start it, but it won't start. Alva is right beside him, but he doesn't see her. He gets out of the car and raises the hood. He comes to the house to get some tools. Now he's trying to fix the motor. Alva looks at me and smiles. She knows that Omar had promised, that morning, to take me for a drive. He hasn't kept his promise yet, and Alva is making signs and gestures to me, making fun of him. Omar gets back in the car and tries again: it won't start. He gets out and calls Rosa, the maid.

They push the car out into the street, trying to start it where there's a hill. They get discouraged and come back to the house. Omar is furious. He hears me laughing.

"Mama, Aurora is talking to herself."

"Leave her alone, Son. Remember, she's frail."

Sick? Me? I've never felt so good! I'm thinking that Omar wants me to be taken to the doctor. He spies on me all the time.

I like my name, Aurora. Alva and Aurora mean the same thing. Mama wanted us to be called Mariana and Anamaria. Papa wanted something more "symmetric," like Alis and Sila, for example. After a lot of arguing, they came up with Alva and Aurora. When Alva would go out to play around the house, I stayed in; when she'd get back, I had to tell her everything that she'd been doing.

"You played in the fountain."

"Yes." I knew because I could feel the wetness in my feet when Alva would splash in the fountain.

The next day, it would be I who'd go out to play.

"You've been eating apples," Alva would say, because she could taste the flavor of the apples when I would bite into them.

When Alva got sick and had to be taken to the clinic, I was left alone at home. Everybody was talking in whispers.

"It's better for you to go to the country," my mother said to me one day.

Those were the saddest days of my life. Suddenly I lost interest in everything. Not even the lovely evenings, with the birds coming back to their nests and singing in the twilight, could hold my attention. It was Alva who could tell one bird song from another.

One day, as I was sitting in the hall and listening to the birds' songs, I heard Alva's voice behind me.

"It's a meadowlark," she said.

And then everything was just as it used to be. We ran through the pastures, we played in hiding places, and, when they left us alone, we climbed trees.

I returned from the country. Mama and Omar were waiting for me at the door. I'd never seen them looking so serious. They took me to the living room and Mama sat down by me. She hugged me and kissed me.

"Aurora," she said, "Alva is dead."

I cried, not for the death of my sister, but for Mama, who was crying, and her grief was contagious.

A few days later, Omar surprised me talking to Alva and he told Mama about it. They took me to the doctor and that's when they started the pills, the shots, and that long train of consultations, when other doctors would come to ask me the same old questions. It seemed as if they all had their heads together and were obsessed with one goal, that I should forget about Alva, which was impossible. When I went to sleep, Alva would appear in my dreams. Omar watched me persistently. This is what I thought: he was jealous. The only person who wasn't concerned about my conversations with Alva was Rosa, the maid. Apparently, our dialogues amused her. She would laugh at us. She would laugh and shut herself up in the kitchen.

Alva and I realized that Rosa was making fun of us. We weren't letting her into our conversations and she thought that was funny. She was laughing at us. "We have to teach her a lesson," Alva told me, and I agreed. Alva and I always agreed on everything except for colors. Her favorite color was blue and mine was red. Mama, who sometimes couldn't tell us apart, let Alva grow her hair long. Mine on the other hand, they kept cut short.

"Aurora," Alva said, "put on your red dress and go tell Rosa that I need her."

When Rosa, answering my command, entered our room, there was Alva dressed in her blue dress with her long hair loose. Rosa went running out of the house. That day she packed her bags and left. Since then, we've never had a maid.

It looks definitely as if Mama and Omar are going to stay home. When the car doesn't start, that's the way it is. Mama hates taxis and Omar is handy.

"Alva," I say in a low voice to my sister, "I want to go for a walk." Alva persuades me to sneak out the window and get to the car that's still parked in the street. We slip down the trellis that goes all the way down to the garden, being careful not to make any noise. Omar has left the key in the car. Alva gets behind the wheel. I'm afraid because I don't know how to drive, but I'm sure that Alva does. She starts the car and pops the clutch. We go down the street at full speed. I see Omar in the rearview mirror, running and waving his arms. Alva steps on the accelerator and laughs.

"Aurora!"

"Alva!"

How beautiful it is to be together!

THE DAMNED

Adolfo Cáceres Romero

Maybe up there, where the air was pure and clean and the village houses farther apart near the foothills of the mountain, there would be someone who would care for her. Someone up in those hills, those staunch phantoms of her childhood. Someone outside of her family. Someone in whom she could redeem herself from the city she was running away from, sick of its evil ways. She searched for the trail where her footsteps had trod so many times; her perspiring body was almost a stranger to it now, she had been absent so long. The clouds enfolded her in their shadows. *"Jump'i."* Someone. *"Jump'i."* She smiled at the thought of that good word, wiping away the tears that glistened on her cheeks. Someone. The thorns scratched her legs.

Time was bringing back some of the strongest memories; she could not wipe out the scars of that city. She couldn't—her boss fondling her furtively in private, her breasts humiliated; the erotic daydreams that would sneak up on her, lying totally still with her fingers twitching between her legs. She couldn't forget the burning desire of her flesh. Her parents, solemn and stone faced, consulted the coca leaves. *"Laiqa, laiqa,* work your magic, work your magic," they repeated. Convulsions interrupted her dream. *"Laiqa, Laiqa,"* and the leaves revealed nothing. Surprise and fear, faces worn with time and superstition, kept watch over the night that was falling around them in a glittering, black mass. *"Laiqa, laiqa."* The coca leaves, saturated with alcohol, were spread over the cold floor. They rubbed the healing ointment over the girl's body. The wind whistled through the grain fields, gently caressing the tresses of the stalks and straw. The blood of a white llama was clotting beneath the fingers pressed against the girl's paralyzed limbs as she lay silent and lifeless. The council of witch doctors pronounced the sorrowful verdict, and the aging parents passively accepted the judgment.

That was the way it had to be—in that death-chant where the activities of the day had ground to a halt. The mourners demonstrated their sorrow with feigned grimaces. The cottage revived its memories with gestures and words that expressed its devotion to the deceased. The deathwatch went on and on until everyone was high on alcohol and coca. It was already dawn when the pallbearers arrived. The shroud slipped from trembling hands and fit her rigid body like a white glove, an aurora of purity. The old ones, her parents, began to weep again as things were made ready for the procession.

The first blows of the hammer against the lid of the coffin made a noise loud enough to wake the dead. At first no one noticed that from within the box were other blows which grew louder and louder in the desperation of their efforts. The hammer seemed to be calling forth a gloomy echo until it finally stopped in midair, paralyzed by the wail that came from inside the box. The mother wanted to move closer to the miracle that was returning her daughter, but she stopped when she saw everyone was turning away terrified, begging the heavens to forgive the damned.

"Condemned!" they repeated.

Suddenly the nails gave way and everyone became silent as the white shrouded figure of the young girl sat up.

"She's been condemned," the whispering murmurs grew louder. The father took the rope offered to him, obliged to save his daughter. "She's damned," they repeated. "She won't be able to rest in peace."

The girl called to her parents and they approached her, their eyes tense as they prayed in silence. "She's damned." The parents cautiously circled the coffin, their daughter, now on her knees, sobbing, imploring. "Condemned." They circled closer. "Condemned." And they could see her pale face, her hands wiping away her tears and reaching out to them.

"Daughter, pray." The father's hands were on the rope, hands with only one will. "Pray, my daughter." His hands were tying a necklace for her.

"Condemned."

The rope turned in hands made to work the land. "My daughter, rest in peace."

The rope constricted the girl's neck until the shroud rested again in silence, and the blows of the hammer resounded once more against the coffin lid.

WILD ANIMALS

Juan Simoni

> *Who puts boundaries on the air?*
> *And who makes himself owner of the river waters?*
> —O. ALFARO

I go down this path looking for the view my grandfather's eyes need to get their fire back. If his eyes keep longing for those valleys, they'll get too cold, and they'll freeze. When my grandfather came to these ownerless mountains, all he brought with him was the little bundle on his back and the eyes of a beaten dog. At first, he seemed all right. But after a while the farm became smeared with humiliation. It smeared his food, the few afternoons when he had a chance to rest, and the long hours of silence. He almost never spoke. The source of the humiliation had a name, Don Justiano, Don Justi, who paid for my grandfather's land with trickery. You see, my grandfather put up the land, and Don Justi put up the trickery, which he had bought from some city lawyers. With a few papers he took my grandfather's little patch of land. It's hard to believe—with all the valleys Don Justi already had for himself!

In these mountains, life isn't easy on anyone. Each day has to be washed in more sweat. If you want to hunt, you have to go out into the woods: no jaguar's going to come to the farm to get his bullet. Keep moving and moving in the woods, the way I'm moving now, among the thorny *carahuatas,* thinking about my grandfather. Some people say that a good hunter always has more than enough food. Sometimes, as a matter of fact, he does, but he never has the time to sit down and eat it, the way God means for him to. You get in the habit of treating hunger rudely and not attending to it when it comes—only when you can. The jaguar doesn't wait. You have to follow it through ravines, up hillsides, along the edges of cliffs, in rain and in sun, by day and by night. But once you're onto its tracks, starting in the regions of Penon Verde, passing the Emboscada del Ganso, and finally going down into the Canon de las Sombras, the jaguar's days are numbered.

In spite of all the hardships, I don't complain. I wouldn't trade this life for any other. Not that I'd say I'm a happy man. How could anyone be happy once he becomes part of the loneliness of these mountains. But I'm not sad, either. When sadness comes, you have to chase it off with a machete so it doesn't settle down inside you and finally take over completely. If sadness comes the way it came to my grandfather, you can't just sit there with your arms crossed. No, sir. You have to scare it off the way you scare the crows when they settle on the fields. If you don't scare them off in time, they stay. They take over everything, and they don't leave us a patch we can call our own.

Don Justi threw my grandfather off his land, and we said to ourselves, "Now he'll leave us alone. Now that the buzzard's full, he'll be satisfied." But one day, as I was skirting the valley and stopped to have a smoke behind some rocks, I heard cries and hoof beats. I looked out over the rocks to see what was going on. It was Don Justi, whipping a man. Don Justi's eyes had those same knives in them that jaguars' eyes have when they meet you face to face. Men's lives are branded in those eyes. The whipped man's crying stopped. Don Justi rode off on his sorrel with its four horseshoes clattering. There's not much to tell: Don Justi had taken the man's lands from him, same as from my grandfather, and when Don Justi came to claim the land, he whipped the man.

Now that he was fatted and owned all the land, Don Justi set himself to guarding it like a sheep dog. Only his animals were allowed in his fields. "My pastures aren't for other people's cattle to get fat on," he said. And even though none of the farmers around had more than a little burro or maybe a cow, it didn't make any difference. Anyone else's animal, if he came upon it, was a dead animal. If you saw a cloud of crows in the distance, you knew for sure that on some farm the people were crying over the loss of their little animal.

I had always thought the forest animals didn't have any owner. But look what happened to my grandfather: he was homesick for the valley, so he went back, and there he killed a deer. Along came Don Justi with all his people and told him, "Goddammit, Anselmo, you know very well you're not allowed to hunt on my property. Well, we're going to have to share this. I'm taking the meat and leaving you the skin."

Time passed. Another day, without thinking what he was doing, my grandfather went down to the valley again. This time he killed a jaguar. Don Justi, who never sleeps, found him: "I told you in no uncertain terms not to do this. Seeing that it's you, I'll forgive you one more time and forget all about it. Now for the sharing. Last time, I gave you the skin. This time, I take the skin and leave you the meat. We'll see if you change your habits at last."

The day finally came when no one could stand in the shade of a tree that belonged to Don Justi.

Now, step by step, I'm getting closer. I know that you get to know an animal as you track it. Some run in a straight line, as if they sense death coming, and you gain steadily on them. Others complicate the chase, bewildering the hunter. They run forward, then back, circle, climb trees, leap ditches, and turn up back where they started. When the moment comes, the final, long-awaited moment, when the circle closes, they let you know who they are: they roar or they crouch low and silent, depending on how close the dogs are. Your finger must never leave the trigger. The smell of rattlesnake fills the air and you hear your heart, oh God, beating faster. But you have to get calm, because one mistake, and you're dead.

And sometimes you can't help damaging the pelt, like that time at the bottom of the canyon. As I was about to cross a stream, my dogs lost the scent, and I lost the track. We came to a halt at the bank. The dogs were sniffing around. A twig snapped. That saved me. From the highest tree the jaguar came down on me. I pulled the trigger twice, and I'm sure the jaguar was dying as he fell, but even so, he left claw marks across my left shoulder. A little closer, and I would have been erased forever from these woods.

And here I am, chewing on the black memories of my grandfather, and moving. A sorrel's hoof prints show me the way. Just beyond this hill is the Aurora Water Hole. If he stops, I'll catch up with him there.

Yes, there he is, watering his horse, It's been a long time since that water quenched the thirst of any living being that didn't belong to him. I look at his body, shaped like a well-fed beast of prey. From the water, which seems to sense its freedom coming, cool air blows. Now it would be easy to pull the trigger, but I must wait until he sees me, until the crows of fear settle in his eyes. Don Justi must know at the precise moment who is killing him and why.

THE STRANGER AND THE SILVER CANDELABRUM

Gastón Suarez

That thief could get away. It all depended on what she said. One of two words: yes or no. He was in her hands. Just one *yes* and that man, whose eyes sparkled with both irony and hope, could go free and on his way again, back where he came from . . . or maybe even, by one of those strange twists of fate, she and he . . .

"Do you know him?"

She shuddered ever so slightly. The harsh voice of the police chief seemed to fit the drab room perfectly—just a table and a chair and on one of the cracked plaster walls the only bit of decoration, an out-of-date calendar with a half-naked woman on it, in color, a young, beautiful woman with well-shaped muscles and haughty breasts. The stares of the police chief, the prisoner, and the two cops who held him increased her anxiety. She wished she could be far away, with her schoolchildren, walking through the fields, delighting in the clean blue of the sky. Nevertheless, here she was, against her will, in order to decide the fate of that man, smiling at her now with a strange rictus.

"I'm sorry to bother you with this, but he says you two are old acquaintances, that you can vouch . . ."

Old acquaintances, yes. Her sharp nose pointed where her eyes were looking—the figure on the calendar. She had looked like that: young, pretty, full of illusions. Many years ago, it's true; but she had looked like that, a little thinner. Her eyes narrowed as she looked at the prisoner. This was the man who had dropped her here into the world where she now lived: a solitary old maid who threw all her maternal love into the children at her school. This was the man who had brought the blood to her cheeks and torn from her mouth the words she had guarded like a treasure: "Yes, I do love you! I will marry you!" This was the one who had left her with the curlers in her hair and the bridal gown on the bed.

"The silver candelabrum is missing from the church, and we found this stranger, but if you know him . . ."

She knew him all right. She had locked up her feelings, and never again would any man manage to make her blush. And now there stood the cause of her distrust and her fear of men. Poor thing, he looked like he had walked a long way. Jesus tells us to forgive. He was so old. But his eyes hadn't lost their sparkle, and his lips—now she remembered well—still had that rictus. She knew him, and just one word from her could save him.

"If he doesn't confess, we have our methods . . . Even the dumb speak with a little urging."

Jesus tells us to forgive. She looked at the calendar. She had looked like that: young, pretty, full of illusions. She had dreamed of her own little house, her three children, her little garden. Jesus tells us to forgive. But what suffering she had gone through there, in her home town. Everyone had laughed at her. She had almost died of shame. She had been forced to take a job as country schoolteacher. She loved the children. She hated men. There stood the cause of her loneliness, her frustration, her bitterness. But she could save him. Jesus tells us to forgive . . .

"Yes . . ."

The prisoner visibly relaxed and breathed a sigh. The cops, with their Mongolian faces, loosened their tentacles and let the stranger's arms free.

"Well, in that case . . ."

Jesus tells us to forgive. But what suffering she had gone through! She had no tears left. Her only pleasure was the schoolchildren, during the day. At night she prayed the rosary and made paper flowers, which she sold to the *campesinos*. There stood the one who had condemned her to this kind of life, where every gray day left her fearful and melancholy, full of gloomy, disfiguring thoughts. There stood the man who had stolen her illusions and the joy she had dreamed of having. If he would only say he was sorry, ask her to forgive him, tell her there was still time . . . if he would at least . . . But no, it was too late. She looked at the half-naked woman. She had been like that. Now, now he was old, tired from walking so far, but with the same sparkle in his eyes and the same rictus on his lips.

"If you know him—"

"Yes, I know him! He's a thief!"

The cops' tentacles grasped the wrists and arms of the prisoner. A cold breeze moved in the cracked-plaster room and flapped the calendar. The police chief and the cops tried to conceal their smiles.

"Zenaida! Forgive me! I came to ask you to marry me!"

The prisoner's words shot from his mouth like weightless butterflies and shattered on her neck. The wind carried off the golden dust of their wings.

It was too late.

She walked back to her school, blaming the wind for the hurt in her eyes. It wasn't tears. No, no. It was the wind. For as long as she had lived in those parts, the wind had caused her an ache in the chest and had irritated her eyes. It wasn't tears. She never cried. It was the wind, the wind.

THAT JUSTICE BE DONE

Oscar Barbery Suarez

Here, Your Honor, we have a grave injustice, and who's the victim? Me! Those people come whining to you, "It's that bald pervert!" And without another thought you get pissed at me. Open and shut case, huh? But drive over to San Javier and ask about me there. Do me that favor, will you. Go to the town I grew up in and find out who I really am. Or if you don't want to go that far, just drop in at the customs house, because they know me there, too, from the boss down to the guys that scrub the grease pots. Ask them. Or talk to the commuters who take the train to Corumba. And if you're still not satisfied, go ahead, ask the girl's mama. Yeah, ask her, but when her old man's not around. She might just tell you the whole truth and nothing but—because the old lady only lies when her old man's around. But you, Your Honor, just get her off by herself, and you'll see. You'll see! She'll tell you how it really happened without subtracting or adding.

But you, my dear Your Honor, nobody's going to pull shit over your eyes. You're a professional! Me, I barely got through high school. I might have been a lawyer like you, but you know how life makes its demands . . . I had to go into business. I realize you don't trust me. I realize that—because you don't know me. But you'll see who's being straight with you. Tell me, in all honesty, do you really think I'd have had to do all that old guy says I did just to get into a fourteen-year-old-kid's pants? I mean, really, Your Honor! What kind of world are we living in? The one thing we got plenty of is women! I realize I'm no Robert Redford, and the women all know that these days love doesn't go in at the ear, either. In the *belly,* my dear Your Honor: a big old cow barbecued for the whole family, and nobody complains about it after. Why should they, goddammit? After they get to stuff themselves, people stay grateful. That's the least they can do. The old man says I raped his daughter. Well, that's bullshit, because the daughter liked to have a good time and she knew how to lead a guy on, with her "Here, Don Ramon. There, Don Ramon. Can I serve you a little coffee, Don Ramon?" You should have seen that little Yuyi, taking her cues from her mother, the way she ran around serving me.

Your Honor, Your Honor, when a man dedicates himself to nothing but his own business and he's a decent man who kills himself working, he thinks everyone's like him and can't believe there are people with nothing better to do than scheme up ways to screw their neighbor, especially when that neighbor had to work hard and pull himself up by the bootstraps. Because here the number one crime is to pull yourself up a little in the world and be different. Let's face it; we all have the same opportunities. And whoever gets left behind, he's only got himself to blame. You, for instance, you wouldn't let anyone steal that degree you got on the wall and let them sign your name, Doctor of Law, because you *earned* that degree, studying, at the university, and God only knows with what sacrifices . . .

That's what people really resent when they know a person. The very same people you grew up with, playing in the pastures, the people that mean most to you—I mean, how can you help not loving the people from your own town? If a stranger badmouths you, well, so what, but when your own people, the people you *thought* were your own, go around doing it, that hurts.

That Sunday, Your Honor, I didn't invite any of that family to visit me. I was out at my ranch, doing what I always do on week-ends, putting my books in order, when they showed up. No sir! They didn't just "happen by" because look who came: the old man, the old lady, sweet little Yuyi, and her two sisters, who don't really count because they're uglier than a poor man's cow—and have calved more, too. But it's a detail that should give you some idea things didn't go exactly the way they're saying. *Now,* of course, they don't remember the big charbroiled steaks they ate in my yard or the three six-packs of beer I had to send for from town for them to drink. Even less they're going to remember the money the old lady borrowed from me and that I never got another whiff of. They don't remember that. But they did go on telling you how I took that Yuyi off to show her around the ranch and that I refused—can you imagine?—refused to let the two ugly sisters come along. Now how were they going to remember all that filled to the gills with my beer? What they wanted to happen, Your Honor, is exactly what did happen; so that afterwards, with a lawyer and judge and all, they could make a grab for the few pennies I got to my name. Well, I did take that Yuyi around, and what happened happened. What's so bad about that? How many times have you probably done the same thing and nobody came to you demanding explanations!

And now don't let them come claiming the kid was a virgin. Your Honor, Your Honor, what kind of world . . . ? Oh, I admit it was nice pretending she was, but that little girl, as you call her, had been around. She had had it with Sancho, Pedro, Martin, and no doubt in my mind she had a steady right there in the neighborhood. There's where you should start your investigation, find the kid who was her steady, the one who knocked her up with no problems for himself, because there was good old Don Ramon to pay the bill. And look how naive I was. When that Yuyi came to tell me she was pregnant, I didn't even think to ask, when did it happen? I felt sorry for her there in my office. She was like a scared animal, whimpering and gulping and crying. Anyone would have felt the way I did, especially someone from the same village. I said I'd help her, and I meant it, with all my heart. If *you* feel sorry for those two peasants when they come claiming that stuff, what about me, their *paisano,* wouldn't I feel even worse? Nobody knows better than me how these people live, the things they have to do to get food in their stomachs and clothes on their backs! There wasn't any way for me not to help the poor kid, who, believe me, had wandered off the straight and narrow a long time ago.

So it all adds up. According to you, I'm guilty of getting that Yuyi pregnant. And oh yeah, not just pregnant, but raped, too, and . . . Your Honor, Your Honor, I don't understand you. How can you make those accusations? I swear to God! My dear Your Honor, let's get the facts straight. I've already told you; sure, I was with the girl, but just one time! There wasn't any rape, believe me. I'm innocent, and the proof is the money I gave to help her out. And not for an abortion! If I *had* thought it was mine, I would've got a good doctor, not a butcher. Problems like that, I don't pinch pennies. If I lose some today, I'll make it up tomorrow. But the way it turned out was that Yuyi—poor dumb bitch—grabbed up the money I gave her, and what happened, God have mercy on her soul, happened.

Yeah, it's clear and simple, as long as you don't look too close. Who's guilty? Don Ramon. Who's got to pay damages to those two old buzzards? Don Ramon. It's not fair! And to top it off, the father—crazy old lunatic—is running around the streets and plazas telling people he's going to chop me up with a machete. And that, Your Honor, that's a death threat. That's a crime. Or isn't it? Not that all his big talk scares me, but you talk to the old man and tell him what's what. Tell him not to make an ass of himself and not to go around telling every Tom, Dick, and Harry he's going to kill me, because if I fall over dead or something, the number one suspect's going to be him. And that's not all. Tell him I've got plenty of brothers who'll go after him if something happens to me. Tell him that. Tell him. Those people'll listen to you. When you think about it, what's that old man really want? To send me to jail and me pay him for the favor? He must really be stupid. And what about me? Who's going to pay me damages for all I'm going through? The old man comes filing charges with you. Who am I going to file charges with? All that guy's going to accomplish is to drive me crazy until I take things into my own hands and settle with him myself, skin for skin. And believe me, he's not going to like that. And wouldn't that look nice for me!

There's work to be done, Your Honor, and I have to be doing it. What this country needs is people who know how to work and bring some progress to this country. And nobody can work with little problems like this nagging at them. It's been five days since I got back from Puerto Suarez, and I still haven't been able to go out of my house to sell the Mercedes I brought from Brazil. Because, as you know, if you don't buy your own seed corn, who's going to buy it for you? Now that the banks aren't giving credit, you have to get it where you can. That Yuyi! Look, Your Honor, I've thought it over. I don't want to complicate my life any more; you take the car. I already told you it's a Mercedes, latest model. Sell it if you like, and give something to those peasants so they can pay their debts, which, they say, are all from their daughter's funeral. And let them have the bishop say a mass for her! Or if you like, my dear Your Honor, give it to your wife, because it's white, and that's the color that really turns women on. Anyway, the car's yours, but take care of this problem for me once and for all so I can sign the registration papers. And do it, Your Honor, as soon as possible, because I'm the one that wants most to see justice done.

MAN ON THE WHEEL

Manuel Vargas

I'd rather not talk about myself just yet. But that's hard. My friends are inside me and I'm in them. My world is the whole world. Life is the same thing over and over. We're in the muck; then we're out of it. Then we're in it again, and in the end, we don't know who got out and who stayed in.

My friend Chino lived in Cochabamba and maybe had it worse than I did. I met him in Ciudad de las Gradas, when we got put in jail. I was scared shitless I'd never get out of there.

"Look here, Rolando," he says to me one night, " I been in jail before. Don't be scared. Take it easy; it's not gonna kill you."

So then I asked him to tell me about it, and he started his story.

Chino was always getting mixed up with women, and he was really good at it. He delivered bread from house to house, and everywhere he went, they got the best of him. I don't know when the whole mess started. Hell if I know! It could have started before he was born. But he said it started the afternoon he met Gloria. That day his whole world was caving in on him. Imagine this kid walking along on Aroma Avenue, down in the dumps, kicking a rock along the sidewalk. Then this Gloria pops up and starts tagging along.

"Hey, brown eyes," she says to him.

He swings around and looks at her, like she was an old car or something. But Gloria, smiling and wriggling, says to him, "I've eaten some of that bread you deliver. Why don't you bring some around to my stand. It's at the corner of La Cancha."

As I've said, my friend was down on his luck that day. So he says to her, "I don't sell bread anymore." And he bows his head and starts to cry.

She stops and takes him by the arm. "What's wrong? Why are you crying?"

He knew then that she was a good woman. She wasn't feeling sorry for him. She'd suffered like he had. "I lost my mother last week. I don't sell bread anymore." And that was all that was said. They looked at each other and walked on down the street, not saying a word, like two old friends.

My friend was just a kid, but with all his troubles, he'd had to grow up fast. Three weeks before that day, he'd started working for a bakery—to help his mother, so she could buy food and dress decent. She liked stylish clothes. At first his job hadn't gone so well. Nobody wanted to pay him for his bread, so he said they could pay later, and he'd started losing money. But no matter, every time the girl down at Don Gerardo's bar would smile at him, things wouldn't look so bad. He lived and breathed for that girl, kept himself cleaned up, and changed his clothes.

Then, his mother died. It was sunny that day, he said, but his debts were hanging over him like a black cloud. He got home and called to her from the patio, but nobody answered. He walked into the front room and found her stretched out on the bed, dead. He passed out and fell on top of her. He was awakened by a pair of cold hands, and saw black figures standing around the body of his mother. His aunt tried to calm him down. The women gave him a glass of *chicha* and something to eat. They were about to leave for the cemetery, and he went along with them, holding his aunt's hand. He was looking at all the people crying, and then he fell down and started snapping like a dog. That's all he could remember. He passed out again; then the fevers and the nightmares started. At least that's the way he told it to me, but I think he got what really happened mixed up with the nightmares.

In a week he got well. He was finally beginning to see what life was all about. His dreams had been doused with cold water. No mother, no house, no job—he could go to live with his aunt, but he wanted to leave, go somewhere, anywhere. When he got his strength back, he went to the cemetery to talk it over with his mother. He thought about his job, his bike, the sun, flowers, his first cigarette. He decided to live down at the bakery. He would work hard, be on his own, become a man. He sat by the grave for a while, not knowing how to cry or how to stop crying, running his fingers over the ground, looking at the shadows of the *molle* trees, and listening to the earth.

Then he started out walking, in no particular direction, and that afternoon was when he met Gloria, the girl who acted like she was an old friend. The next day Chino's life changed. He left his bike down at his aunt's house, threw his stuff into a bag, and went to work down on Angosta Street. For the next two weeks, all he did was deliver bread. Later he learned to do everything. At night he made the dough with Angel—who turned out to be a pervert. In the morning, he would deliver bread to his old customers. In the evening, he would go to Cala-Cala. He and Angel would sleep under the table, snuggling up together to stay warm.

And what happened to Gloria? Well, my friend went to La Cancha several times, but she wasn't at any of the stands. Time passed, and he gave up hope of finding her. One night, Angel showed up drunk and put his arms around him, and they jerked each other off. Chino went to Cala-Cala every day, and thought about Gloria. He fantasized about her smile, her trembling breasts, her brown thighs and hips. He bought a pack of cigarettes and learned to smoke. He started crawling into the corner at night to get away from Angel. He had nightmares and couldn't sleep.

Sometimes in the afternoon, he'd pass by La Cancha. Soon he decided he wasn't ever going to find Gloria. His mind was a blank. He couldn't imagine her face anymore, her smile, or her hands. Could Gloria have been just another hallucination, like the ones he'd been having since his mother had died? Why couldn't he remember anything but her hips and thighs and all that part? What had she done to him? What a fine way real women had of treating a man! They'd get you in their clutches and then disappear.

The rainy season came. One night, Angel didn't show up. They all had to work harder, and they finished late. The boss and his wife, Doña Elisa, went to bed; Chino was left alone under the table. Half an hour later, he heard footsteps and nearly screamed when he felt the old woman's hands touching him.

"Have you got room under there, Chinito?"

The devil take her. She wanted to take advantage of my friend. There was scratching, hugging, fear and loathing, until finally they both fell asleep without doing anything.

The next morning, Chino got up feeling sleepy and tired; he was disgusted with the whole business. He started thinking about the past few months. In the beginning, it'd been all nice; he'd tried to dress nice, eat right, and work hard. Now he was all skinny and ragged. He rode around on his bike, half asleep. He didn't dare look at Don Gerardo's girl. She still looked at him, but not like before.

Many times he dropped his basket and bread spilled out into the street. He ran into trees and got chased by dogs; once he ran over a beggar who ran after him, cursing and throwing rocks.

That morning he got hit by a car. He suddenly found himself lying in a heap of tires, baskets, and loaves of bread. He got up and picked up the bread. He fixed his bike as best he could and got on. Two blocks down the street he started feeling pain in his back and hands. There was blood on his forehead, and his bike was making squeaky noises. He had to stop beside one of the stands, and there stood Gloria.

"Would you like to buy some bread, ma'am?"

She opened the door and walked out. "So, you've finally come. You sure know how to make a body wait!" she said smiling.

He realized he couldn't say a word or get off his bike. She touched him gently on the arms and on his forehead.

"You're all beat up! Did you get run over? You can't work like this. Come in here; let me put something on those cuts."

Muscles tense, lips trembling, my friend looked like a statue of a worker on strike. She fixed him up so well that, when she'd finished, they were able to give each other a little kiss, and two days later, he was out selling bread again. What a great time they had. He got up earlier than he had to and went to the stand, so they could talk and laugh. They talked about love, and then he said, "Listen, didn't you tell me you were living with your mom?"

"No, my parents are separated. I just live with Papa, but at night I'm always home by myself."

"Where does your father work?"

"I'd rather not say."

"Why not?"

She just laughed and touched his cheek. "No reason. He works at night and hardly ever comes home to sleep. Listen, try to get here earlier tomorrow if you can. About four."

He said he would and then left. And as he peddled along on his bike, he thought, "Women are so strange . . ."

That night they finished the kneading early, so by three o'clock he was walking through the deserted streets. When he got to La Cancha, the first stoves were being stoked for the *api*. It was misting, and steam was rising up from the shadows. Drunks were sleeping or singing at every other street corner. The dark figure of a man came toward him from a narrow street. With his coat collar turned up and his breath steaming the cold air, the man looked like a giant to Chino. They came face to face.

"Where'd you get this bread?" the man asked in a monotone.

"From the bakery on Aroma Avenue," Chino answered, a little shaken.

The stranger picked up a round loaf, sniffed it and bit off a piece. "Not bad," he said, chewing it. "Not bad."

My friend watched him while he ate, looked at the narrow slits of his eyes, his greasy skin, the black scarf that stretched from his neck to his belly.

"I'm a policeman," he mumbled, wiping his mouth with the scarf. "This is good bread. I'd like you to take some over to the police station. But I need to know the name of the baker so I can draw up a contract." Chino was trembling. "Did you hear me?" the man yelled, and Chino nearly jumped out of his skin. "I'll be waiting down at the square at ten o'clock. Ask for the chief of police."

"Yes, sir."

The man smiled and stalked away, like a lion. Chino, able to breathe again, wanted to head straight to the stand, but he could feel someone watching him from behind. When he got to the door, he looked around before knocking. The man had stopped to watch him.

"Where are you going?"

"To Lanza Street," Chino answered, and he kept walking.

He couldn't go back to the stand. He felt like the policeman was still standing there ready to ask him where he was going. He couldn't get the man's bleary eyes and dirty scarf out of his head. He wasn't about to go to the police station. His boss had told him not ever to tell the police where he'd gotten the bread, and if they ever did ask him, to give the name of any other bakery. Why had he been told such a thing? Was it against the law to sell bread?

How was he going to find Gloria? He had an empty feeling in his stomach; he didn't feel like doing anything, not even delivering bread. He got off his bike and sat down on a bench and started to cry; he didn't give a damn about anything. He was just going to sit there until he got tired, and then . . . and then what? He looked over at the chapel of the Corazonistas. A crowd of people were going inside for Sunday mass. He could hear the choir singing a hymn in Quecha. He wanted to throw rocks at the people, so they would turn around and see him standing there, nearly naked except for his sorrow . . . but he just kept on crying.

Quite a few days later, he went to Gloria's stand. When he told her what had happened, she just laughed at him. Chino was confused, but eventually things returned to the way they'd been before. He and Gloria agreed again to meet earlier the next day.

At three o'clock in the morning, Chino was knocking at her door. Gloria appeared and guided him inside.

"Aren't you cold?" she asked.

"Yes."

"Come over here."

He followed her to a corner of the room. "Where's my bike?" he asked.

"Don't worry."

They drew close together and began to feel each other's warmth. She touched her face to his. "Chino, do you love me?"

"I love you."

She offered him her lips, first gently, then kissed him so hard it hurt. He felt his strength leaving his body. They caressed each other all over, and she arched her body until she fell back on a stack of ponchos.

At least, that's what he told me.

After that first time, they lay still for quite a while. Then he started to caress her breasts, and she began to sigh, and the whole thing started again. They kept on like that. He thought he'd found a reason to go on living. Imagine that. Over and over. And every time he got turned on, life seemed like an eternity till he could rid himself of his juices and flop down like a piece of pressed sugar cane, happy to know he could fill up again, never run out, come to life and die, come to life and die . . .

The trees along the avenue were losing their leaves, the wind had begun to blow, and it was getting colder. One afternoon Chino was riding along on his bike, dressed in a bright shirt and slacks. All he needed was a pair of boots and a red tie. He thought about the first spring rain, the fresh smells, the clean streets. One time, at the beginning of the May twenty-fifth celebration, he'd found a ten-thousand-peso bill and thought about buying himself a red tie. That was the morning—or had it happened before then—that he'd met the girl at Don Gerardo's bar. Strange. He never even thought about her anymore. She was barely a dream. A person dreams a lot in the spring. Now he had a real woman. One afternoon, he'd found his mother dead, and he'd forgotten about the tie. Now he was headed to where his mother lay. He rode through the big cemetery gate, the grounds where the rich folks were buried, the gully. He stopped under the shade of a *molle*. He didn't feel sad anymore. He remembered the promise he'd made in that same place, one afternoon, and was glad he'd kept that promise. He was a full-grown man now.

He got up, went out of the big gate, and climbed back on his bike. He thought back to when he'd first started selling bread, door-to-door, how scared he'd been, weaving in and out of the cars, and how he'd had to beg the women to buy his bread. "Someday I'll be like a lion in the jungle," he'd said to himself back then, and now he was.

Time passed. Angel and Chino became friends again. One talked about Gloria, and the other, about Doña Elisa.

"That old woman is a bitch," Angel said. "All women are bitches."

Chino trembled with rage. But finally they poured themselves a glass of *chicha* and went on eating their fried pork. They were in Cala-Cala.

The boss was the same as always: working hard, never opening his mouth, and getting fatter every day. Now he had five boys selling bread for him.

The first time Chino asked Gloria to go out for a walk was on a Sunday. That was the day he put on his new, bright-colored clothes and went to wait for her down at the square. He leaned up against the white bridge railing and smoked a cigarette. The creek below was dry; the wind ruffled the locks of his slicked-down, black hair. He looked up at the church towers and began to pace nervously. Yellow leaves were strewn along the paths. He reached La Esquina and saw her coming down San Martin. She was walking along, carrying a white sweater in her hand, and wearing a pink mini-skirt. She came close to him. She'd put on lipstick and perfume. They caught the number three bus and rode away, sitting in the same seat. Outside, the wind was twirling the leaves around.

They rode along, holding hands as the bus passed through eucalyptus trees. Sitting next to Gloria, Chino felt like a man. When they got tired of riding, they stopped to sit down by a canal. When they talked, it was just foolishness; it was more fun just walking along, pinching each other. The dead leaves blew past in little whirlwinds, and rain was threatening.

Only skeletons of leaves were left now along the street. Chino kept on waking people up to sell them bread. He'd go to Gloria's stand first, and then he'd cover the whole town. One morning he knocked at the door of Gloria's stand but no one was there. What could have happened? Why hadn't she let him know? Was she sick? Out of nowhere came the image of her face, smiling bitterly. He walked away, deep in thought and rubbing his eyes. The whole day went badly for him. The next day he arrived even earlier, but no one was there. What could have happened to Gloria? And that afternoon, he went by La Cancha again, only to find the door still locked.

Time went by. One day, one of the women who worked at La Cancha handed him a note. Gloria had written, with a shaky hand, for him to go to the stand at five the next morning. He got there at half past four and no one was there. But soon two faceless men appeared, surrounded him, and grabbed both his arms. Somebody wanted to see him down at the police station.

They put him into a cold cell; he could hear people walking around, doors and drawers being closed, and people coughing.

"No, Papa," he heard a woman saying. "No! I don't know who it was, but don't do anything to him."

The guard came and told him to get up. They went into the other room. In the middle of the room, behind a desk, was the man in the dirty scarf. Sitting next to him was Gloria with her big stomach sticking out.

The man in the scarf couldn't believe his eyes. His hands were shaking and he was about to jump out of his chair. Chino said she'd done him dirty. I don't know if she had or not, but he said he was sure of it. The man in the scarf looked at the guard, who went over to Gloria and led her out of the room. She never once glanced over at my friend. Chino and the man stood staring at each other, without saying a word. Imagine that. Then somebody knocked at the door.

"Can I send the next one in?"

"Adelante!"

Then the baker came in, wearing his apron all covered in flour.

"Get this bum out of here; give him a year in jail," he roared, and spit on the floor.

The guard went over to Chino and put the handcuffs on him. Then two more men went over and started pushing him out the door.

That's how he ended up in jail. That's where he finished up becoming a man; "Thanks to a bitch," he used to say. First he got a whole day without a bite to eat, and then a night on the dirt floor, the next day, the kicking and all the rest. That's the way it is on the inside. I know because I was with him after that, in the jail at Ciudad de las Gradas. That's how they make a man out of you, by treating you like an animal. That's the way it is now.

Later on, Angel went to jail, too. He told my friend he'd reported the boss for illegal sales so he could have the old woman all to himself. But the boss bribed the chief of police, and the one who ended up in jail was Angel.

Chino was miserable thinking about the year he had ahead off him. But once he and Angel got together, they started planning their escape. I think they started digging a hole in the cell wall. I don't know if they really got away or if they were just released in a year. Chino didn't get to finish the story; they moved him to another cell, said he was mixed up in something political. But anyway, he managed to get out the first time, and ended up here, where I met him. By then, he was a woman-chaser if I ever saw one. The two of us went to jail together. He knew his way around by then; I was still wet behind the ears.

And here's the end of my story. Just to brag about myself a little, let me tell you about my situation. I'm in jail now for the second time, and next to me sits a new guy, who shakes even in his sleep. And when he wakes up, I'm gonna tell him how I got put in jail the first time. And then he'll do the same thing for the next guy, when he comes along. That's what we're alive for, going around and around, like a wheel, and who knows where the hell it's going.

I'm not sure whose story I've told, mine or my friend's. It really doesn't make much difference. If anybody finds a way out, a way to break the circle, tell him to come see me. I'm in San Pablo Prison, second patio, cell eighteen, Ciudad de las Gradas, which happens to be the capital of my country: headless, footless, and half plowed under.

CONTRIBUTORS

GERMAN ARAÚZ has had stories published in journals in Cochabamba, La Paz, and Santa Cruz.

NICOMEDES SUÁREZ ARAÚZ was born in 1946. He writes in both Spanish and English and has been published in the United States and Latin America in various literary journals. Two of his works are *The American Poem* and *Caballo al anochecer.*

GUSTAVO CARDENAS AYAD is the author of *Tiro de Gracia,* a collection of short stories.

YOLANDA BEDREGAL (1892–1916) was an essayist and professor. Her works appear in various anthologies and include *Almadía, Del Mar,* and *La Ceniza.*

HOMERO CARVALHO was born in 1957. He has been awarded literary prizes in Bolivia and Mexico. Among the works he has had published are *Biografía de un otoño,* a collection of short stories that appeared in 1983, and *El Rey Ilusión,* a children's book published in 1984. He has also had many short stories published in numerous anthologies.

VIVIANA LIMPIAS CHAVEZ was born in Santa Cruz in 1963. She writes poetry, short fiction, and drama. Her works include a book of poems, *Bajo un sol ajeno,* and one of short stories, *La Espera* (1987).

ALFONSO GUMUCIO DAGRON was born in La Paz in 1950. He is a poet, an essayist, and a fiction writer; his works of fiction and poetry have appeared in numerous anthologies and literary journals. In 1970 and 1971, he was in charge of the cultural section of *La Ramon,* a morning newspaper. He was a columnist for *La Ultima hora* and has been a collaborator in numerous anthologies published in Bolivia and Mexico. He has two major books of poetry: *Antología del Asco* (1979) and *Razones técnicas* (1980). In 1982 he received the Testimonio Award from the Instituto Nacional de Bellas Artes for his essay concerning the coup of July 17, 1980; he has also written a significant historical work, *Bolivia* (1981).

JULIO DE LA VEGA was born in 1924. He is perhaps one of the most well known Bolivian poets of this century. His poetic works include *Ampliacion Tematica,* 1957; *Temporada de Liquines,* 1960; *Poemario de exaltacion,* and others. His work has been included in numerous anthologies.

ROLANDO PAREJAS EGUÍA was born in 1963 in Santa Cruz. He is a younger poet of literary renown; his works have appeared in numerous anthologies and literary journals. He was the promoter of a literary workshop in Santa Cruz and is editor of the literary quarterly *Borrón.*

REYMI FERREIRA was born in Santa Cruz in 1965. He has studied law and has been a representative of the Federacion Universitaria Local (Universidad Autonoma "Gabriel Rene Moreno"). He has two major collections of poetry, *Querer el cielo de adentro* (1985) and *Entró temblando el amor* (1987).

AMILKAR JALDÍN was born in Santa Cruz in 1956. He writes both poetry and short fiction. He has won the Casa de Cultura Raul Otera Reiche literary prize, and his work has been published in various journals. He is also an actor in the theater.

OSCAR BARBERY JUSTINIANO was born in 1929. He is a lawyer, a diplomat, and the author of several novels, including *El hombre que sonaba* and *El reto.* His main collection of short stories is called *Su hora mas gloriosa.* He is the father of Oscar Barbery Suarez.

ALEJANDRO MARA was born in Buenos Aires of Bolivian parents in 1956. He has resided in Santa Cruz since 1988. Professionally, he is a journalist; his works have been published in various journals and periodicals and in cultural publications sponsored by literary organizations of Santa Cruz. His major work is called *Espuma vertical.*

EDUARDO MITRE was born in 1943. Poet, essayist, and critic, he recently edited an anthology of contemporary Bolivian poetry: *Poetas Contemporaneos de Bolivia,* with an annotated critical introduction. His poetic works include *Elegia de una muchacha, Morada, Ferviente humo, Mirabilia,* and *Razon Ardiente,* a bilingual Spanish-French edition.

RAMON ROCHA MONROY was born in 1950. He is an attorney and a university professor who writes short stories and news columns; he writes for the newspaper *Los Tiempos.* His principal works include *Hora cero,* 1976, and *El Padrino,* 1979, both collections of short stories, and *El Run Run de la calavera,* a novel.

WALTER MONTENEGRO was born in Cochabamba in 1912. He is well known as a journalist and author of several books of political theory and collections of short stories. Some of his major works include *Once cuentos, Los Ultimos; Introduccion a las teorias politico-economicas;* and *Oportunidades perdidas: Bolivia y el mar.*

ROBERTO ECHAZU NAVAJAS was born in 1937. He is a poet and an essayist whose work has been published in numerous anthologies and journals. Main works of his are *1879* (1973), *Akirame* (1966), and *Triptico del hombre y la tierra* (1969).

RENATO PRADO OROPEZA was born in 1937. His works include books of criticism, collections of short stories, and novels. His collection of stories *Argal* shared the Cochabamba 1967 Science and Literature Prize with Adolfo Cáceres Romero. His 1969 *Los Fundadores del Alba* won both the national Erich Guttentag Novel Prize and the Casa de las Americas Prize, the most prestigious literary prize in Latin America; it has been translated into English as *The Breach.*

PAZ PADILLA OSINAGA was born in Pampa Grande in 1961. A short-story writer and novelist, he has had several short stories published, including "Nel umbral" (1986–87), "El Gemido del huracán" (1991), "Los Jinetes del tiempo" (1992), and "La Covacha del loco" (1993). His most recent work is a novel, *El Ogro Miope* (1995). He has won two national literary awards, UTO-85 and España-90, and is presently working on a collection of short stories.

ELIAS SERRANO PANTOJA was born in Cotoca, a province of Santa Cruz, in 1948. He writes poetry and short fiction. His poetic works include *Poemas de amor y vida* and *Caminos de niebla.*

BLANCA ELENA PAZ was born in Santa Cruz, Bolivia, in 1953; she studied nursing in La Plata, Argentina. Seven of her stories are included in *Taller del Cuento Nuevo,* stories by writers from the Santa Cruz region of Bolivia (1986). She is now working on her first collection of short stories.

ANTONIO ROJAS is a poet whose works have appeared in various journals and anthologies, including the *Antologia Provisional: Poesia Joven de Santa Cruz,* 1986. His main work, *Cantico,* was published in 1985.

ADOLFO CÁCERES ROMERO shared the Cochabamba 1967 Science and Literature Prize with Renato Prado Oropeza.

FREDDY ESTREMADOIRO ROMERO was born in Santa Cruz in 1953. He has written short stories and poetry, and he paints. He resides in Camiri, where he is an educator.

LUIS ANDRADE SANJINES was born in Sucre, Bolivia, in 1949. He now resides in Santa Cruz. Poet, essayist, and artistic critic, he is part of the group of artists known as "Grupo de Artistas libras" and the literary group "Uno son suficientes." His book, *El Loco de las Flores,* has been published, and his work has appeared in various anthologies and literary journals.

GERMÁN COIMBRA SANZ was born in 1925. He is a poet, an essayist, and a playwright. He was the first to receive the Juegos Florales Marianos award in Santa Cruz, and he is also a recipient of the Jazmin de Plata award in that city. Among his works are *Mientras tanto* and *Romances del camino,* both books of poetry, and *Diego de Mendoza,* a critical work on historical drama.

PEDRO SHIMOSE was born in 1940. He is a critic, a poet, and a fiction writer. He has had numerous poems, essays, and major works published, including *Triludio en el exilio.* His poetry has appeared in many anthologies.

JUAN SIMONI, a native of Charagua, in Santa Cruz, Bolivia, is a geological engineer who has lived in Argentina, Peru, Venezuela, and Mexico. He has had one volume of short stories published and is at work on a novella.

GASTÓN SUAREZ was born in 1928 and died in 1984. He left the legal profession to dedicate himself to literature. His major works of collected fiction are *Vigilia para el ultimo viaje,* 1963, *El Diario de Mafalda,* 1975, and *El Gesto,* 1969; he has a dramatic work, *Vertigo o el perro vivo,* 1975, and a novel, *Malku,* 1974.

JORGE SUÁREZ, born in 1932, is considered by his contemporaries to be one of the most significant Bolivian poets of his time. Together with Felix Rospigliosi, he is the author of *Hoy Fricase.* Other poetic works of his include *Elegia a un recien nacido,* 1964; *Sonetos con infinito,* 1976; and *Oda al Padre Yunga,* 1976. His work has been included in practically every major anthology since the 1950s.

OSCAR BARBERY SUAREZ was born in 1952. He is an architect by profession, and he is a former literary editor of the Santa Cruz newspaper *El Paiz* and the creator of the popular Bolivian comic strip *El duende y su camarilla.* His drama *Porta Voz* was produced on stage and television, won first prize in the 1987 National Literary Competition for the Theater, and was published as a book in 1988.

ALCIRA CARDONA TORRICO was born in 1926. She is called a social poet by critics such as Yolanda Bedregal, Juan Quiros, and others. She has served in the Dirección de Cultura de la Alcaldia Municipal de La Paz and obtained the "flor natural" award in the Juegos Florales sponsored by the Rotary Club of La Paz. Her works include *Carcajada de estano, Rayo y simiente,* and *Tormenta en el Ande.*

JESÚS URZAGASTI was born in 1941 in El Chaco. He was director of the magazine *Sisifo* and for some time was in charge of the cultural page of the *Presencia,* a newspaper in La Paz. His poems have appeared in various literary journals throughout Latin America. His works include *Cuadernos de Lilino,* a book of prose poetry; *Yerubia;* and *En el país del silencio,* a novel that was translated by Kay Pritchett and published as *In the Land of Silence* (University of Arkansas Press, 1994).

MANUEL VARGAS was born in Vallegrande in 1952. He studied literature in La Universidad Mayor in San Andrés of La Paz. He is a short-story writer, novelist, and author of children's books. His major collections of short fiction include *Cuentos del Achachilla* (1975), *Cuando las velas no arden* (1980), and *Cuentos de Ultratumba* (1982). His *Los signos de la lluvia,* a novel, was published in 1978, and another novel was published in 1980: *Rastrojos de un verano.* His stories have appeared in numerous anthologies, and he continues to write and work in La Paz.

RUBÉN VARGAS was born in 1959. His poetry has appeared in numerous anthologies; his main work is *Señal del cuerpo,* published in 1986.

BLANCA WIETHÜCHTER was born in 1947. Her poetic works include *Asistir al tiempo* (1975), *Madera viva y arbol difunta* (1982), *Territorial* (1983), and *El Verde no es un color* (1990). She is one of Bolivia's prominent women writers. Her works have appeared in numerous anthologies and literary journals, and for years have been published in the journal *Presencia* of La Paz.

RENZO GISMONDI ZUMARÁN was born in 1967. He is a poet, a short-story writer, and an artist. His artwork, poetry, and fiction have won numerous awards and have appeared in various journals of art and literature. He had a volume of poetry published in 1993.